WHITEWASH

WHITEWASH

Exposing the health and environmental dangers of women's sanitary products and disposable diapers— what you can do about it

LIZ ARMSTRONG
ADRIENNE SCOTT

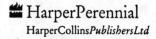

HarperPerennial
HarperCollins*PublishersLtd*

Text and cover stock, 100% chlorine-compound free paper

The authors express their sincere appreciation to the Margaret Laurence Fund for the Promotion of Peace and the Environment for its invaluable support of this book.

First Edition

Canadian Cataloguing in Publication Data

Armstrong, Liz
    Whitewash

Includes index.
ISBN 0-00-637709-2

1. Chlorine — Toxicology. 2. Chlorine — Environmental aspects. 3. Sanitary supply industry — Environmental aspects.
4. Wood-pulp — Bleaching — Environmental aspects. 5. Paper products — Health aspects. 6. Paper products — Environmental aspects. I. Scott, Adrienne, 1959- . II. Title.

RA1247.C5A7 1992   363.73'84   C92-093368-8

92 93 94 95 96 ❖ AG 5 4 3 2 1

To the Rachel Carson in all of us

Contents

Preface and Acknowledgments

This was supposed to be a coffee table book filled with exquisite photographs of natural things, but somewhere along the way it became a paperback about women's sanitary products.

Just beyond our back door here in rural Ontario is an ever-changing world of wonders. Its gifts are especially plentiful and inspiring in spring (what winter-weary Canadian doesn't long for spring?) when everything is impossibly green and spangled with dew, those "gems of earth and sky begotten," as George Eliot wrote. Breathtaking. Along with at least three million other amateur photographers, I often fantasize about capturing and sharing some of these gentle but surprisingly sturdy little miracles in an elegant book.*

Then, in the spring of 1990, along came Bernadette Vallely, co-founder and director of a vigorous British group called the Women's Environmental Network. Bernadette was

*There are many such books already, of course. One of the most inspiring, in our opinion, is *The Sense of Wonder*, with text by Rachel Carson (best known and understandably revered for her world-wakening *Silent Spring* in 1962) and photographs by William Neill (published by The Nature Company).

one of several outstanding keynote speakers at the conference Women and the Environment: Charting a New Environmental Course, held in Toronto during late May 1990. Intense and inspiring in her vision, and not at all afraid to chide us North Americans for our excesses, Bernadette later mused aloud about the possibilities of a Canadian version of WEN's book, *The Sanitary Protection Scandal*. "Is there a writer in the house?" she asked. Who could say no to someone so compelling? I put down the camera and picked up the pen.

The fact that this book is about women's sanitary products is—from one perspective—almost irrelevant. It is our way of expressing deep concern about "the environment," of doing something more than composting our kitchen waste, separating bottles, cans and newspapers, and worrying about worlds of wonder everywhere that continue to deteriorate. From another perspective, it *is* about time we broke the silence about all those disposable sanitary products we so discreetly consume and discard by the billion.

The fact that this book was written at all is thanks to Adrienne Scott, environmental lawyer and researcher extraordinaire, who offered her help in late 1990 and was instantly elevated to co-author. She soon swamped both of us with enough paper to start our own recycling depot—scores of scientific studies, articles from obscure journals, even a few pieces in Swedish and German (which made nearly as much sense as some of the ones in English). Wonder woman!

Many aspects of this subject are dauntingly scientific and technical. Several kind individuals did their best to put it all into plain language for us, but Renate Kroesa of Greenpeace rose above the rest. From beginning to end, she was the source of answers to our most bewildered (and bewildering) questions, and the soul of patience.

We thank all those who read our many drafts, too numerous to mention (readers *and* drafts); Linda Rosier for keeping us on an even keel; Jacques Bourbeau (Adrienne's covivant) for putting up with home-style sanitary product experiments; our project group of Miriam Wyman, Marjorie Lamb and Elizabeth Lamb (yes, The Lamb Sisters) for their ongoing encouragement; Allison Meistrich for picking up so many of the little pieces; and the enthusiastic crew at HarperCollins, including editor-in-chief Iris Skeoch for her very useful suggestions, copy editor Mia London for ironing out the many wrinkles in our prose, Laura Krakowec for so graciously incorporating endless changes, and Stan Colbert, who decided to publish this book because it's time *someone* did.

And to Rip the dog, who had to forgo more than a few walks in those lovely woods while we struggled with the intricacies of organochlorines.

LIZ ARMSTRONG
Erin, Ontario
November, 1991

Introduction

With your help, a whole new chapter in the environmental movement is about to begin. The focus—are you ready?—is women's sanitary products. That's right—tampons, sanitary napkins and those inane little items called panty liners.

Are we crazy? Maybe. But before you dismiss this idea as totally preposterous, read on, at least for a few more paragraphs.

In early 1989, a British group called the Women's Environmental Network released a small book, published on a shoestring, called *The Sanitary Protection Scandal*. Together with a really good publicity campaign, the impact of this little book was stunning. It described the environmental and health implications of the production, use and disposal of "sanitary" products and disposable diapers, particularly those bleached "whiter than white" with chlorine gas. In response, women from across the United Kingdom took up their pens in alarm. They wrote more than fifty thousand letters to manufacturers and members of the British parliament demanding changes to paper products of all kinds, but especially to diapers and the so-called feminine hygiene products.

Then, astonishingly, in just six weeks, all the major British sanitary protection companies—with the exception of tampon manufacturers—had promised to mend their ways, to abandon the environmentally hazardous chlorine gas bleaching process. Six weeks!

Here was the proof that women have astonishing power to act for environmental change. Even the campaign organizers were happily thunderstruck by this unexpected and energetic response to their call for action. Such an impressive environmental coup was no accident, but the result of at least three factors that converged simultaneously:

- First and foremost, the target audience was right. Women are deeply concerned about the environment and its continuing deterioration and are prepared to act to protect it.
- Second, the British campaign provided a clear focus for this wide-ranging concern. Many women are seriously worried about environmental degradation but feel overwhelmed by the sheer number and enormous scope of such problems as global warming and the depletion of the rain forest. But the Women's Environmental Network set a specific target—chlorine-bleached paper products. And not just *any* of the numerous chlorine-bleached paper products, but primarily women's sanitary products. Despite the hush-hush, semi-clandestine aura that continues to hover around menstruation in general (what century is this?), women's sanitary products are still an obvious target for collective pressure from women. It's about time.
- Third, along with describing problems associated with chlorine bleaching, campaign organizers also provided excellent suggestions for taking action.

And over and above all these factors was the secret weapon—women's consumer power. Although we don't own much of the world's wealth—a mere 1 percent, in fact—women do most of the shopping—more than 80 percent. This is enormous clout if we choose to use it. You can bet the British sanitary protection manufacturers were deeply worried in early 1989 that they were going to pay a hefty price in reduced profits unless they eliminated chlorine gas, and fast.

Given the swift success of Britain's "chlorine-free" sanitary product campaign, we think this feat is well worth repeating in North America. We can use our own consumer power to help get rid of chlorine in pulp and paper bleaching, and not just chlorine gas, but all chlorine compounds. In turn we will help purge the world of a serious toxic chemical problem.

What is this problem? The pulp and paper industry's practice of bleaching pulp "whiter than white" with chlorine produces a large class of chemicals known as organochlorines, some extremely persistent and toxic, which include the infamous dioxins and furans. These toxic compounds have been at the center of a furious debate by scientists, environmentalists and countless others. It's a controversy like no other in science. In our first chapter, we describe chlorine's Jekyll-and-Hyde role in our twentieth-century lives. The case for banning the thousands of industrial applications of this volatile chemical is growing more convincing every year. And the pulp and paper industry is an obvious place to start.

At the same time, we don't want to mislead or frighten you. Chances are probably slight that feminine hygiene products bleached with chlorine are hazardous to your health, although trace levels of dioxins and furans have been found in them. Unfortunately, far too few tests have been carried out on women's products—many more have been done on coffee filters and disposable diapers—so we can say nothing for certain (except, of course, that any possible problems could be totally eliminated just by cutting out chlorine).

But even if feminine hygiene products themselves probably aren't dangerous, the wastewater cascading from chlorine-bleached pulp mills contains enough organochlorines to add substantially to the destructive burden of poisons already in our environment. Together, their effects are particularly threatening to the most vulnerable of us all: developing infants and children.

The truly absurd part is that chlorine bleaching is totally unnecessary—who needs a bright white sanitary napkin? Pulpmakers say that bleaching with chlorine also purges contaminants and improves the absorbency of pulp somewhat, but there must be a better way. And there is, says Renate Kroesa, a chemist from Greenpeace.

Beyond introducing you to organochlorines, other chapters in this book are devoted to the giant North American pulp and paper industry—we might as well know what we're up against—and each of the sanitary products that have so long been shrouded in secrecy. Then we move on to disposable diapers, perhaps the most notorious consumer product of the late twentieth century. (A friend wonders what our descendants who excavate our garbage dumps will think of this apparent ritual of packaging infant excrement in bulky, plastic-coated wrappers. Was this a form of offspring worship? Was this meant to be our gift to the ages?) While disposable diapers are not feminine hygiene products, women do buy most of them, and they're really quite a story (*and* a burden). Although we don't specifically address the issue of adult incontinence pads in our book, the "graying" of North America and our addiction to disposables ensures that this is a rapidly growing segment of the sanitary product market. Virtually everything we conclude about throwaway diapers bleached with chlorine also goes for incontinence products.

The main priority of this book is to inspire women to demand chlorine-free sanitary products in North America. That's the first step. But single-use sanitary products, like disposable diapers, also create a substantial waste problem. They squander forest resources and contribute to our growing mountain of garbage. And those tiny little tampons—so easy to flush away—turn out to be another great big headache. Aside from the waste problem, a number of other health and safety issues are associated with tampons and sanitary napkins.

All this leads us down the path to reusable sanitary products. (We hear a few groans of protest already, so enough said for now.) Chapter 8 explores the idea of reusables in more detail and, by the time you get there, you may be more than ready to give them a try. If it makes sense for diapers, why not feminine hygiene products?

But we also have another motive for doing this book. We want to plant a seed that will encourage women to do more to help heal the environment. And we want the emphasis on working *together*.

No doubt you're already doing plenty on your own—composting kitchen garbage, taking your own bags to the supermarket, packing "garbageless lunches," leaving the car at home and using public transit or cycling. All of these small acts of environmental kindness are urgent and necessary, a big step in the right direction. But even multiplied millions of times over, they won't be our salvation. Take tree planting, for example. Virtually every save-the-Earth book we've read describes planting trees as an excellent way to combat global warming, because trees absorb carbon dioxide, the main greenhouse gas culprit. This is true, so keep on planting. But to offset all the carbon we spew into the air by driving cars (the worst offender) and running countless other gas-powered and wood-burning devices, we each have to plant *880 trees* annually, according to the American magazine, *Garbage, The Practical Journal for the Environment.* The greenhouse gas problem is much larger than the most ambitious tree-planting program ever proposed anywhere in the world, larger even than the billions of trees promised by American President George Bush. (And lest we forget, the trees have got to stay in the ground for tree planting to work its magic. The reality is that the world's forests continue to be sliced down at a frightening and unsustainable rate.)

Here's a quick question: In your opinion, what single problem poses the gravest threat to the environment? Many people say it's the population explosion, which will probably double our numbers here on Earth to about ten billion by the year 2050.

But another problem—perhaps more menacing—is our extravagant lifestyle. According to Alan Durning of the Worldwatch Institute in Washington, "The richest billion people in the world (which certainly includes us) have created a form of civilization so acquisitive and profligate that the planet is in danger. The lifestyle of this top echelon—the car drivers, beef eaters, soda drinkers and throwaway consumers—constitutes an ecological threat unmatched in severity by anything but perhaps population growth." The richest billion are responsible for over half the greenhouse gas problem, more than 90 percent of ozone-layer destruction, most toxic chemical contamination and on and on.

Basing his assessment on the results of a worldwide energy study, Durning goes on to say that the Earth's entire population, at least at its present level of just over five billion, could survive sustainably if we utilized renewable energy technology to its absolute fullest extent and—very crucial—if we lived our lives like moderate western Europeans. That means we would live in comfortable but modest homes, use standard conveniences such as refrigerators and stoves, and have good access to public transit, "augmented by limited auto use."

However, Durning goes on, "The entire world population decidedly could *not* live in the style of Americans, with their larger homes, more numerous electrical gadgets, and auto-centered transportation systems." (Canadians belong in this spoiled, self-indulgent category too, of course.) We really are in danger of succumbing to our excesses. Is this our fate? Will we literally shop till we drop?

Some say that too much of the burden for "fixing" our environmental woes already falls to women, overworked as we are with full-time jobs, families to feed and clothe, and all that laundry we hang out on the line to save electricity. So a book beseeching women to do even more for the environment undermines our quest for equality. Right?

Not necessarily. The idea is not to exhaust ourselves with more unsung physical labor (we've surely had enough of that), but to draw on a fresh source of power—our collective consumer clout—to bring about some really useful improvements, starting with sanitary products and diapers. This, we hope, will lead to a whole series of "next steps" that will transform our deep concern and anxiety about this beleaguered old world into even more pressure for change. But the first step we must definitely take is to stop consuming so much. We need to say no thanks to more superfluous stuff. How many pairs of Nikes do we need? Do we really need an extra appliance, a second car or a four-bedroom house? Enough is enough!

Impossible situations can change—and they will, if we set our hearts and minds to it, and *work together*. Recently, a group of Sudanese women, faced with the prospect of a nuclear-waste dump landing on their doorstep, sang for ten days outside government buildings in Khartoum until the decision was changed. Yes, they *sang*, despite all of the other unimaginable problems—famine, civil war and dire poverty—confronting them daily.

When we were growing up in the 1950s and '60s, our parents used to tell us—especially when we didn't eat our vegetables—how lucky we were to be living in this limitless "land of plenty." Well, we've been on a binge ever since. It's time we started using our consumer clout to demand safer, more durable products. It's time we *stopped* consuming as if there's no tomorrow. And there may not be one if we keep on squandering the future at the rate we're squandering it now.

What better place to begin than with women's sanitary products?

1
Chlorine:
The curse of
bright white paper

"Whiter than white" is an old advertising chestnut that conjures up images of pristine purity and cleanliness. But, while it might still apply to laundry, it's passé for pulp and paper products. Why? Because the principal agent of paper's dazzling whiteness—chlorine—is guilty of creating some of the most toxic pollutants ever discharged into our environment.

Chlorine is a chemical Dr. Jekyll and Mr. Hyde. In pure form, it's a highly reactive, yellowish-green gas. On the one hand, it is widely used to "cleanse" drinking water and treat municipal sewage. On the other, it's the noxious vapor that sentenced soldiers to grisly deaths by suffocation during the First World War.

Pure chlorine is never found in nature because it's so volatile it immediately hitches itself to any substance conveniently at hand. Gaseous chlorine is strictly a human invention, first introduced in the late nineteenth century and mass-produced by breaking the sodium and chlorine bond in one of the world's most plentiful natural substances—sodium chloride, commonly known as salt.

Elemental chlorine was and still is widely used as a bleaching agent and disinfectant. But it really came into its own during the Second World War, when industry began synthetically joining chlorine with organic matter, combinations of carbon and hydrogen atoms that are the building blocks of all life on Earth. These experiments opened the door to a whole new realm of chlorine-based chemical products, and to a whole slew of hellish new poisons.

A crystal-clear explanation of man-made organochlorines—how they work, why they're so poisonous and persistent—is found in the early pages of Rachel Carson's 1962 classic, *Silent Spring*, the book that breathed life into the modern environmental movement. Carson explains that the principal objective of these wartime experiments was to create chemical weapons far more lethal than the simple chlorine and mustard gases of the First World War. Because many of the laboratory trials were carried out on insects, when the war was over, these organic potions were turned with a vengeance—where else?—on agricultural pests.

The fledgling pesticide industry grew in leaps and bounds during the late 1940s and '50s. Ever-increasing amounts of chlorinated substances with names like DDT, endrin, dieldrin and chlordane were sprayed and dusted on farm crops, gardens and forests, where they began their invisible, insidious march into every nook and cranny of the living world, including human tissue. *Silent Spring* sounded an eloquent warning about the onslaught of chlorinated organic compounds, citing a steady procession of deadly effects on wildlife and their habitats. In short order, these potent synthetics were endangering fragile balances that had taken nature millions of years to perfect.

But pesticides are only part of the picture. The entire chemical industry mushroomed in the post-war period, exhibiting a cocky confidence about its ability to bend and manipulate nature for the convenience of humans. Front and center in this meteoric rise was chlorine, which now reaches into so many aspects of our late twentieth-century Western lives that it's stupefying. Combined with organic substances—usually petrochemicals—chlorine plays a key role in a multitude of products, including plastics, paints, dyes, bleaching agents, cleaning solvents, aerosols, deodorants, refrigerants and wood preservatives. Moreover, it is central in the manufacturing process of materials such as rayon and cellulose. When the five-billion-dollar-per-year North American chlorine industry says this substance is "interwoven into the fabric of our lives," it's not exaggerating.

But along with the products comes a dizzying list of pollutants, including many of the world's most intractable. Some organochlorine products yield extremely hazardous wastes when they're manufactured; others discharge poisonous by-products when they're consumed; still others release toxic substances when they're burned. Chlorofluorocarbons (CFCs) are poking large holes in the ozone layer. Polychlorinated biphenyls (PCBs), used widely as electrical insulators and still abundant despite being banned in the 1970s, wreak havoc on wildlife by interfering with reproduction, causing birth defects and depressing immunity. (Beluga whales in the St. Lawrence River are so badly contaminated with PCBs that their bodies are declared hazardous wastes when they die.) Chlorinated solvents contaminate our groundwater. Even using ordinary, chlorine-based household bleach, which is a dilute solution of sodium hypochlorite, produces trace amounts of chloroform, a known animal carcinogen and a suspected human carcinogen. And the litany goes on.

Some organochlorines are sheer accidents, the unwanted by-products of other processes. The notorious chlorine-based dioxins and their close relatives, the furans, fall into this "accidental" category. When chlorine gas is used to disinfect municipal sewage, a process still widely believed to be harmless, it also yields a batch of chlorinated chemical "accidents," many of which are highly toxic.

And this brings us back to whiter-than-white paper. Here, chlorine is the key ingredient used by the pulp and paper industry to bleach wood, to strip out its naturally brown organic molecules, leaving pure cellulose, the prized forerunner of whiter-than-white paper. The result? Another batch of "accidents"—not just dioxins and furans, but as many as a thousand or more assorted organochlorines, including some well-known carcinogens and mutagens. These end up in the pulp effluent, in the air, in the "sludges" left over when the solid gunk settles out of the process wastewater. And they get into the paper products themselves.

Over the years, only a handful of the most noxious chlorinated organics, including several condemned by Rachel Carson, has been banned or severely restricted. DDT, PCBs, chlordane, Silvex and 2,4,5-T fall into this category, although, hypocritically, we still manufacture DDT in North America for export to other countries. CFCs are also on their way out, scheduled to be eliminated by the year 2000. But many of the highly problematic compounds are still being produced—by design or by accident—and they're exacting a heavy price from our ecosystems.

What is it about organochlorines that makes them so odious? Here's a quick rundown:

- Most of the chemicals produced by forging new bonds between chlorine and organic substances are brand new to nature. They resist breakdown and are often very slow to decompose, in some cases taking years or decades. Some actually break down into *more* toxic substances once in the environment.
- Organochlorines are often hydrophobic and lipophilic. That is, they hate water and love fat, which is bad news for living creatures. Most do not readily dissolve in water, but instead gravitate toward fat-containing organisms where their persistence allows them to "bioaccumulate" as they move up the food chain. Dioxins and furans in the tissues of some fish species, for example, have been measured at one hundred and fifty thousand times greater than their level in the surrounding water.
- They're excellent hitchhikers, carried everywhere by atmospheric winds, river systems and ocean currents. This accounts for their widespread presence in once pristine environments like the Arctic. Some water-borne organochlorines have been found fourteen hundred kilometres downstream of their pulp mill of origin.
- While some organochlorines *do* occur naturally in the environment, with a few exceptions, they're produced on a very small scale and serve very precise functions in the host organism (for example, they might act as an antibiotic). Industrially produced organochlorines, on the other hand, are almost completely foreign to nature. Still, they may be similar

enough to naturally occurring (unchlorinated) substances to "trick" living organisms, some of which can't easily detoxify or eliminate them. One theory about dioxin, for example, is that it mimics a steroid-like hormone. Masquerading as these hormones, it fools the body's standard chemical response into setting off a variety of physiological effects.

- These effects include suppressed immunity, damage to major organs such as the liver, reproductive and developmental impairment, infertility, birth defects and cancer. Rainbow trout have experienced delayed mortality (death twenty-eight days after exposure) and changes in growth and behavior at the unimaginably low dose of thirty-eight parts per quadrillion of dioxin, which in numerals looks like this: 38/1,000,000,000,000,000.

Some environmentalists believe the case against chlorine is so overwhelming that the only solution is to totally phase out the industry, with all its forty million tons of products per year. As preposterous as this may seem at first—even Rachel Carson didn't rule out all pesticide use—there is growing pressure in Europe and from several environmental groups here in North America, among them Greenpeace, Pollution Probe and Great Lakes United, to do just that. "We think the best and only place for chlorine is back in salt," says Burkhard Mausberg of Pollution Probe in Toronto, adding that any proposed phaseout will have to be carefully planned to protect jobs and give chemical corporations time to introduce safe alternatives, many of which are already available. But the pressure on the pulp and paper industry to "get the chlorine out" is much more immediate and is coming from a host of organizations, some very broad-based, including the Pulp Pollution Campaign, headquartered in B.C., which counts paper and woodworkers, consumers and women's groups among its fifty-four members. Greenpeace's agenda calls for paper companies to be "chlorine-free by '93," while Pollution Probe has set 1995 as its goal for the paper industry.

We too are aiming at the shorter term with our more modest objective: to rid the pulps used to make women's sanitary products, disposable baby diapers and incontinence pads of *all* chlorine and chlorine-based bleaching compounds as soon as possible.

Any discussion of chlorinated pollutants discharged by the pulp and paper industry into our air and water sooner or later gets around to one particular substance—the dreaded dioxin. Described by one science writer as "the Darth Vader of all synthetic chemicals," the mere mention of dioxin touches off an avalanche of controversy. Few toxic compounds have inspired so much fear and loathing, and none has sparked such intense and costly scrutiny from the international scientific community. Greenpeace estimates that two *billion* dollars has already been spent to unravel the mysteries of this single substance, with no end in sight.

Dioxin isn't just a chemical—it's a bewildering political, economic and scientific Pandora's box. All the information we collected—hundreds of articles and documents, although just a fraction of the total in print—was loaded with conflicting "facts," endless figures, daunting science and plenty of smoke and mirrors.

Yet as mesmerizing as dioxin is, we want to stress that it is far from the whole reason we're committed to getting the chlorine out of women's sanitary products, diapers and incontinence pads. As Renate Kroesa, chemist and researcher with Greenpeace in Vancouver, explains, "Dioxin is just the tip of the iceberg really. An estimated one thousand chlorinated organic substances are formed during the process of bleaching pulp with chlorine gas and other compounds like chlorine dioxide and hypochlorite. Dioxin is quite easily eliminated from the picture—or at least reduced below detectable limits—but that still leaves us with a batch of organochlorines, many of which we know very little or nothing about. The majority haven't even been identified yet. Those we do know include harmful substances, such as chloroform and carbon tetrachloride, that are tightly regulated when discharged by other industries."

But this "tip of the iceberg" is certainly fascinating.

Dioxin bombshells began dropping on the paper industry in 1987. That year, public interest in this substance surged after Greenpeace released a confidential American Paper Institute report stating that trace amounts of the most dangerous dioxin, the 2,3,7,8-TCDD variety, had been found in everyday consumer products such as disposable diapers, sanitary napkins, tampons, toilet paper, coffee filters and cigarette papers. The first shockwaves hit in August 1987, packaged in a report called *No Margin of Safety* by the Oregon-based team of Paul Merrell and Carol Van Strum. This investigative gem described how pressure by the American pulp and paper industry on the U.S. Environmental Protection Agency had kept the lid on a known dioxin problem for at least four years. No attempt was made by the industry or the EPA to curtail or eliminate dioxins in the pulping process until after *No Margin of Safety* was released.

Dioxin is actually a family of seventy-five related organo-chlorines, the most toxic of which is 2,3,7,8-TCDD, or tetra-chloro-dibenzo-p-dioxin. How powerful are these dioxin chemicals? To date, they have proven to be the most potent of all synthetic poisons. Tom Webster, a researcher with the Center for the Biology of Natural Systems at Queens College, New York, explains: "They cause a whole spectrum of effects, including cancer, birth defects, atrophy of the thymus, liver damage, reduced immunity, reproductive failure, skin disfigu-ration and weight loss. Although the outcomes may vary from species to species—and are hotly contested in humans—the dioxin-like compounds are some of the most toxic and potent cancer-causing agents ever evaluated."

This is not a gentle substance, so it's not surprising that the American Paper Institute first tried to prevent public disclo-sure about its presence in pulp effluent. When that failed, however, the focus shifted to public relations and image con-trol in an attempt to downplay dioxin and its effects. Numerous tactics, ranging from the sublime to the ridiculous, have worked quite well by, if not defusing public opinion, then at least confusing it sufficiently to neutralize criticism.

One ploy used by the industry is to point out just how tri-fling dioxins, furans and other organochlorines are—in-finitesimal fractions buried in the cascade of total pulp tonnage and wastewater. After all, this argument goes, these toxins only add up to a few parts per trillion or quadrillion. But because we cannot really comprehend such miniscule amounts, the pulp and paper industry helps us "understand" by transferring these fractions to another context: "For per-spective, one part per trillion is the equivalent of one second in 32,000 years, one part per quadrillion is the equivalent of one second in 32 million years."

Time is a neat way to trivialize the numbers. In its context, such tiny fractions of course *do* seem inconsequential. But consider a perspective surely much more relevant to the issue. The vitamin B_{12} is essential to human life. We can't survive without it. Our daily need for B_{12} is 10 parts per trillion relative to our body weight. While this is a very minute amount, it is certainly not insignificant. As dioxin pioneer Dr. Douglas Hallett explains, "The reality is that when you're dealing with poisons or essential nutrients, the so-called 'infinitesimal amount' is what makes or breaks it." Remember our example of the rainbow trout.

Another strategy the pulp companies have used is to point the finger at other sources of dioxin. They claim this chemical isn't just *their* problem. Instead, they fix the blame for dioxin emissions on the burning of toxic waste and municipal garbage in incinerators, leaded gas in cars, smelting copper, preserving wood with chlorine-based chemicals and even on "naturally occurring" sources such as forest fires. (Dioxin from forest fires is at best dubious—Great Lakes sediment studies have shown no measurable levels of dioxin before the 1940s when the chemical industry began large-scale production of chlorinated organics.) Or they simply say, "dioxin is everywhere." (True, of course, because dirty industrial processes combined with those amazing environmental mixers known as wind and water transport it far and wide.) But these excuses are an irresponsible cop-out. All of these other sources do emit dioxins. However, we think the pulp and paper industry, which uses about 14 percent of the chlorine produced in

North America, should only be concerned about its own discharges, and should be doing its best to reduce them—all the way to zero.

The industry's ace in the hole is that it's impossible to verify scientifically that the grievous health problems dioxin causes in the laboratory actually occur in the real world. So when Adam Zimmerman, chairman of the giant Toronto-based corporation, Noranda Forest Inc., claims that "nobody has been hurt by this stuff [dioxin] in a pulp mill," he can safely cloak himself in the rigid armor of "scientific proof." In fact, *anyone* can rightly argue that dioxin from pulp mills—or anywhere outside the laboratory—has never been scientifically proven to cause such problems as cancer, birth defects, reproductive problems and so on. But buyer beware: smoking has never been scientifically proven to cause lung cancer either, yet according to a recent Health and Welfare Canada report, one in five Canadians died prematurely of smoking-related illnesses in 1989.

However, let's give the North American pulp and paper industry its due. Since 1987, it *has* taken several steps to decrease dioxins and furans in paper products and pulp mill effluents—in some cases reducing them below detectable levels—and to reduce the total discharge of organochlorines.

How has it done this? The key strategy has been to try to change the process by replacing chlorine with chlorine dioxide, which produces fewer organochlorines. A few mills are now using oxygen in the first stage of bleaching. Further, contaminants in the raw wood chips and pulp defoamers, like magnets to the volatile gas, have been reduced to a minimum. And most of the mills that didn't have them before are adding huge outdoor lagoons that temporarily trap the pulp wastewater and treat it biologically, breaking down some of the chlorinated wastes with microbes.

But still more problems. The principal cure prescribed by the industry to reduce dioxin, substituting chlorine dioxide for chlorine gas, is not proving to be trouble-free. It produces a different breed of chlorinated by-products, one being chlorate, a well-known herbicide that can wipe out aquatic plants around a mill's outflow pipe unless it's subject to a great deal of treatment.

When mills have applied these abatement measures diligently, total organochlorines have dropped substantially, by as much as 50 percent or more. But look at it this way, the volumes being dumped were so huge that *any* progress would be welcome. This is still a dirty industry, and is still a long way from eliminating its chlorine-based pollutants. The 150 Canadian and U.S. pulp mills using chlorine still dump about one million metric tons of chlorinated organic material into rivers, lakes and oceans every year. This is a loathsome price to pay for "whiter-than-white" paper products.

But it's not necessarily the quantity of effluent that matters, it's the toxicity, how poisonous the discharges are in the environment. And there's a substantial difference between *acute* effects, the short-term killers, and *chronic* effects, which develop following continuous low doses over long periods of time. Chronic effects are much more subtle, but can still threaten the survival of species, tripping off reproductive problems, physiological changes, deformities, cancers, mutations and so on.

With progress being made at reducing organochlorine discharges, the industry is making some rather stunning claims about toxicity. The Pulp and Paper Research Institute of Canada (PAPRICAN) states that reducing the load of organochlorines discharged per tonne of pulp below a certain level "knocks the socks off the toxicity" of the effluent, decreasing it by 90 percent! According to one PAPRICAN researcher, the magic number is 2.0 kilograms of AOX per tonne of air-dried pulp. Although we've tried to avoid technical terms, this one is important. AOX stands for Adsorbable Organic Halogens, and roughly represents the amount of chlorine (which is a halogen) present in a mill's effluent.

But these claims are challenged by most people in the scientific community. Why? Far too little is known about the content and qualities of bleached mill waste. Low weight organochlorines are of particular concern because they can pass through biological membranes, the cell walls in living organisms. Science says only 10 to 40 percent of these compounds have been assessed for their environmental toxicity, so we're still largely in the dark about them. With this amount of uncertainty, it seems premature for PAPRICAN to make such extravagant claims.

Have bleached pulp mills been successful in reducing toxicity? Although we have no definitive figures for American pulpmakers, the forty-seven Canadian mills using chlorine were scrutinized in a federal report released in November, 1991. It concluded: "Seventy-five percent of Canadian bleached mills discharge effluents that are acutely lethal, and even after dilution by the receiving waters, seventy percent of the freshwater bleached pulp mill effluents are still within the range of chronic toxicity. The chronic effects observed downstream of Canadian bleached pulp mills include significant irreversible factors which jeopardize the continuance of the species and the integrity of the ecosystem." About half of these mills operated secondary treatment facilities at the time this study was conducted. And while the report strongly recommended that *all* Canadian mills install secondary ponds, this caveat was added: "It should be noted, however, that wastewater treatment leads to the generation of sludges which contain large amounts of chlorinated organic compounds for which as yet no monitoring or disposal strategy has been developed."

Even extremely low levels of organochlorines, less than half the rate claimed to "knock the socks off toxicity" in Canada, are causing problems at Swedish mills. Scientists there have observed a variety of problems with aquatic animals, such as damaged mussel shells and deformed shrimp eggs. And evidence is also emerging in Canada showing that even highly-treated pulp bleaching effluent can cause decreased growth and reproductive damage in fish.

Even if you are impressed by the industry's claim that dioxin has been reduced to "non-detect" levels in bleached pulp effluent, remember three things: first, that "non-detect" doesn't mean zero; second, few pulp mills have consistently achieved non-detect yet; and third, that yesterday's problems with dioxin will be with us for a long time. Where the most potent dioxin, 2,3,7,8-TCDD, was regularly discharged into the environment by pulp mills using chlorine, there *is* a lasting and troublesome legacy. Shellfisheries in nine areas along the British Columbia coast, for example, are all closed "until further notice" because of high dioxin counts, and many of the estimated 30,000 to 50,000 toxic dumpsites in North America are laced with this persistent poison.

The truth about chlorine, in any form used by the pulp industry, whether gas, dioxide or hypochlorite, is that it's impossible to contain within the pulp manufacturing process. Truly environment friendly "zero discharge" pulp mills operate in a closed loop, recycling all of their pulping and bleaching chemicals. But this is impossible with chlorine, because—as a chemical relative of salt—it's too corrosive. You can try to reduce how much you put into the process, and you can try to solve it at the end of the pipe with secondary treatment ponds, but pulping and bleaching with chlorine will never be pollution-free because it cannot be contained, at least not with today's technology.

Add all of this to the other common pulp mill pollutants such as aluminum, zinc, lead and mercury, plus masses of fiber particles, and a more complete picture of pulp mill effluent starts to emerge. (And these are just water pollutants, not air emissions such as sulfur dioxide. Kraft mills also emit foul-smelling hydrogen sulfide and toxic mercaptans.) Even the best effluent control systems cannot begin to eliminate them all.

Had enough? Many of our ecosystems have too. In heavily populated regions such as the Great Lakes and the Columbia River basin, a slew of pollutants from other industries join the pulp mills' toxic leftovers. And still more contaminants are contributed by sewage treatment plants and pesticide-laced water runoffs from farms.

The Great Lakes, depressing to say, are one of the best places in the world to study the health consequences of toxic compounds, especially organochlorines. Dr. Jack Vallentyne, senior scientist at the Canada Centre for Inland Waters in Burlington, Ontario, points out that seven major reports written since 1978—six of them joint efforts between Canada and the United States—have examined the connection between toxic chemicals and the health of vertebrates in the Great Lakes basin. Their conclusion? "Toxic chemicals, in large part organochlorines, have impaired or are impairing the health of natural populations of fish, reptiles, birds and mammals. The concentrations of organochlorines in these wild populations are in the same general range as those found in humans. Because of their short generation times, populations of fish and wildlife may be showing effects that will appear later in human populations. On this basis and direct evidence from a limited number of human studies, the reports also concluded that there is a clear threat to human health. The dimensions of the human health threat are not known." What *is* known, Dr. Vallentyne adds, is that "the children of individuals exposed to persistent toxic chemicals, including organochlorines, are at far greater risk than their parents."

Several research projects have focused on new mothers who regularly consumed quite ordinary quantities of Lake Michigan fish—between one to three and a half fish meals per week. These fish had accumulated significant burdens of several toxic substances from the lake, mainly PCBs but also other organochlorines. A review of this ongoing work—much of it done by Dr. Joseph Jacobson and Dr. Sandra Jacobson of Wayne State University, and Dr. Harold Humphrey of the Michigan Department of Health—was reported by Dr. Wayland Swain in the journal *Aquatic Toxicology*. Although scientific language can be difficult to understand at times, his summary is clear and succinct:

Effects observed among infants born to [these] mothers ... include delays in developmental maturation at birth. These infants were smaller in physical size, had reduced head circumferences, altered lability of state [instability], increased startle reflexes, and were classified by attending physicians within the "worrisome" neonatal category.

Dr. Swain, now vice-president, U.S. Operations, of Eco-Logic International Inc. in Ann Arbor, Michigan, rounded out the picture when he testified in late 1989 before the environmental assessment hearing evaluating the giant Alberta-Pacific pulp mill near Athabasca, Alberta. These babies "were immature autonomically.... Their motor systems were immature. They moved in a jerky cog-wheel fashion, rather than the normally fluid movements you would expect. They responded to changes in their environment more poorly.... They were duller than their unexposed counterparts."

Because their mothers' breast milk showed higher concentrations of toxic organochlorines than the control group's, scientists at first hypothesized that breastfeeding was principally responsible for the babies' problems. But a study of the same children at four years of age, published in the January 1990 issue of the *Journal of Pediatrics*, proved that these problems originated in the womb rather than as a result of breastfeeding, because observed "deficits" weren't related to the amount of contaminated milk consumed. The authors stated that, "*in utero* exposure to PCBs and related contaminants is associated with poorer short-term memory functioning in early childhood.... Although there was no evidence of gross functional impairment at the levels of exposure, the poorer memory performance seen in the study indicates diminished potential."

The mothers of these children also suffered health problems. They tended to be anemic before and during pregnancy. Many experienced swelling—edema—while carrying their babies, and they were more susceptible to infectious diseases.

What makes results of these studies particularly alarming is the fact that PCBs have been banned since the 1970s, long before these infants were even conceived. Dr. Swain puts forward the theory that even though levels of PCBs have declined by a factor of five—there is five times less now than fifteen years ago—what remains is more toxic than the previously sizeable inputs. He points out that wildlife in the Great Lakes region is now suffering greater difficulties—increased mortality of eggs, major birth deformities, actual disappearance of several species—despite the sharp reduction in PCB levels.

Incidentally, at the Alberta-Pacific pulp mill hearing, Dr. Swain also reported declining sperm levels in North American men, which he said decreased dramatically in 1975, and had "crashed" by 1980. "What is the cause? Frankly, I can't tell you, and I don't know anybody that can. But what I can tell you is that the 1975 and the 1980 values were strongly associated with toxic organic contaminants measured in the seminal plasma, the fluid that surrounds the sperm cells. And the correlations were quite striking." Acknowledging that his data did not necessarily prove cause and effect, Dr. Swain added, "But what I can tell you is that very critical human tissues are becoming affected by these toxic substances. And this is not a special population at risk. This is the average of North American society."

One-hundred and seventy-seven organochlorine compounds have been detected in humans, and these are ordinary Canadians and Americans, not special populations exposed to higher doses of toxic chemicals, such as native peoples dependent on a diet of contaminated fish, or workers in industrial plants handling chlorinated compounds or effluents. And even though chlorine-based substances like PCBs and DDT have been banned, our body burdens continue to rise as a result of pollutants dumped into our ecosystems from a variety of sources, including bleached pulp mills.

And we can't save ourselves simply by avoiding obvious exposures, such as meals of Great Lakes fish. "Persistent toxic substances contaminate all food by virtue of cycling through the air, land and water," the Great Lakes Science Advisory Board states. "Our bodies, like those of other organisms, are parts of the cycle."

Some scientists argue that organochlorines from pulp mill effluent simply aren't in the same league as PCBs, because there are far fewer of them by volume. Quite right—they're not. But our contention is that it's sheer madness to add more organochlorines to the existing pool of PCBs—and the entire organochlorine mess as a whole—especially where opportunities exist to eliminate some sources altogether. And we believe the pulp and paper industry is an excellent candidate.

Dr. Rosalie Bertell, mathematician, peace activist and director of the International Institute of Concern for Public Health, says "species deterioration" should be of grave concern to all of us. "If we damage offspring by massive pollution, they will be physically less able to cope with life than their parents. At the same time we are dumping thousands of old and new chemicals into air, water, land and food, giving them a much more hazardous world to cope with. This is a death process—slow and torturous."

North American pulp and paper manufacturers are not the worst offenders, but they do dump enormous amounts of chlorinated organics into our waterways, and they are significant contributors to this needless "death process." We've been born and raised to believe that whiter than white is better. But we now know beyond doubt that when it comes to paper products, bright white is dirty and dangerous. Although corrective measures have been tried at both ends of the pulp production pipe, the only fail-safe—and surely the most obvious—remedy is simply this: get the chlorine out.

2
Pulp, paper and other consuming passions

Products lining supermarket shelves are an interesting barometer of what's happening on the environmental front. There you can see how pressure to "walk lightly on the earth" takes shape in the products offered to mainstream consumers.

Toilet paper is a good if surprising example. Rarely an item that earns much glory, it's currently one of the "green" leaders at the grocery store. More toilet paper is now made from environmentally correct 100 percent recycled paper than any other household tissue product. Reams of the stuff have materialized in supermarket chains across the continent this past year, prompting more than one consumer to wonder, "Recycled from what?" (This question is not necessarily facetious, since many goods with "recycled paper" labels on their packaging contain miniscule amounts of what really counts, post-consumer waste.)

Shelves traditionally crammed with bright white chlorine-bleached household paper products are now making way for a few other token recycled and unbleached items, such as Scott Paper's new tissue line, offering several products in two versions: unbleached fibers for western Canadian consumers, and recycled for easterners.

But take a closer look at the shelves: the bulk of household tissue products are still the traditional "whiter-than-white" chlorine-bleached type (even if many *are* dyed to match decors). Across the aisle, women's sanitary products and disposable diapers are stalled in a similar environmental backwater, even more oblivious to change. While these products cannot be made with recycled fiber—at least not yet—they certainly could be chlorine-free. And aside from the bleaching issue, waste is an obvious problem with tissue and sanitary products—they all make a one-way trip to the landfill site or municipal incinerator.

Although many North American pulp and paper companies have recently been hustling to clean up their act, this industry has historically been one of the world's dirtiest. For decades, pulpmakers polluted almost at will, especially in Canada where the credo, "the solution to pollution is dilution," is still the operative philosophy at some mills. Despite latter-day industry pledges of its undying commitment to the environment, much of the "greening" has been prodded by pressure from European customers, negative public opinion and threats of government regulation. And when it comes to the specific task of getting the chlorine out, most North American pulpmakers have settled for half-measures.

The pulp and paper sector *could* teach the world a wonderful lesson in the art and science of being clean and green. Paper is unique: it's a natural product, fully biodegradable, recyclable and made of a potentially renewable resource. While there are a few mills that have put environmental excellence right up there with earned profits, on the whole, the industry has a long way to go. As Greenpeace says, "Short-sighted forestry practices combined with ecologically damaging production technologies and wasteful consumption habits have turned paper and its manufacturers into a hazard to the environment and human health."

"Wasteful consumption habits" is putting it mildly. We don't have to look very far back to realize how besotted North Americans have become with paper products. In the years before the Second World War, we each consumed about 130 to 150 pounds of paper per year. Five decades later, our consumption—and with it, the pulp and paper industry—has exploded. "In overall terms, the seventy million tons of annual U.S. production, together with seven million tons of net imports, translate into 640 pounds of paper and paperboard consumption for each man, woman and child in the country," the American Paper Institute proudly boasts. Five times more than the pre-war period! Canadians aren't far behind, consuming about 20 percent less paper per capita than the average American.

Another look at those supermarket shelves confirms what the statistics say: we're the world's biggest paper gluttons, even if household paper products represent just a fraction of total use. But it's simplistic to blame consumers for all this excess. Totally needless packaging accounts for much of our consumption. And consumers didn't dream up the notion of transforming trees into paper diapers, paper towels, paper table napkins and so many other single-use disposables, including those dreadful drinking boxes kids take to school in their lunches. (Apparently, they can be converted into park benches but what percentage of these little sinners are actually saved? And how many more park benches do we really need?) It was manufacturers and marketers who concocted all these paper products, and then drowned us with advertising and promotions. Good consumers that we are, we simply bought them—along with all the clever marketing lines—in sufficient quantities to create endless mountains of paper garbage. Nearly 40 percent of our landfill waste is paper.

Consider this: if everyone on earth used as much paper as we do in North America, the impact would be devastating, an ecological nightmare. We asked John C. Ryan, a World-watch Institute research associate specializing in forestry issues, to describe the consequences: "If everyone in the world—all 5.5 billion of us—consumed paper and paperboard products at the same rate we do here, logging for pulp would increase over seven times. Overall, loggers would have to cut almost three times as much forest as they do now. The environmental degradation that usually follows from logging would undoubtedly increase by a similar amount. Since forests and other ecosystems are already straining under the pressure of the world's demands, it is inconceivable that they could support increases of this magnitude."

Yet even with the world population expected to mushroom to over six billion people by the year 2000, North American pulp and paper producers don't seem too worried about forest degradation. They're too busy looking for a hefty share of the new business. "Paper and plenty of it will be required to meet the needs of men, women and children the world over, as their cultural and social standards improve," says President Howard Hart of the Canadian Pulp and Paper Association.

In mid-1991, thirteen billion dollars worth of new pulping operations were on the drawing board or under construction in Canada to help meet this expected surge in demand. In the United States, eighteen mills were expanding capacity and six new plants were in the works.

It's depressing to contemplate the future of our forests once these new mills and plant expansions are operating at full tilt. Industry claims it is doing a good job of "managing" North American woodlands, but critics say we're a long way from practicing sustainable forestry.

Forestry Canada's latest figures (1988) show that just over 80 percent of the area harvested or lost to fires and pests was successfully "renewed," compared to only 63.6 percent a decade earlier. These renewal figures sound heartening, or at least a step in the right direction, but over the twelve-year period from 1976 to 1988, Canada's so-called "productive" forest decreased by an area almost as large as Prince Edward Island. And despite timber shortages in many provinces, Forestry Canada said a case could be made for increasing harvest levels, at least in the short term.

A note about "renewal", which sounds nice, but is something of a misnomer. Renewal practices fall pitifully short of restoring the forest to its natural richness and biodiversity. Harvested areas are usually restocked with only one or two varieties of fast-growing trees, while soil-replenishing species such as aspen and alder are frequently destroyed by herbicides so they don't interfere with the growing crop of merchantable trees.

Environmentalists call Canadian forest practices "a national scandal." "We are facing a crisis equal to the Amazon," says

Colleen McCrory of Canada's Future Forests Alliance. "Without public debate, without environmental hearings, and without proper studies, Canada's forests are being transformed into pulp and exported. This huge giveaway will destroy entire ecosystems." Even the majority of Canada's professional foresters range from lukewarm to disgruntled in their opinions of woodland management—73 percent rated it either "fair" or "poor" in a recent Forestry Canada survey. Sixty percent said the government allows too much timber to be cut.

In the United States, more seedlings are planted than trees are cut down every year, but the last remnants of wilderness are still under siege—less than 5 percent of the ancient forest survives. These "old growth" tracts, which existed when the first European settlers arrived in the seventeenth century, are found mainly in the Pacific Northwest, Oregon and Washington, and Alaska, where they continue to be heavily logged despite widespread and vocal opposition.

The Native Forest Council, a group of concerned private American citizens who want to preserve what remains of the country's old growth ecosystems, says the "rate of destruction is difficult to imagine, but picture a line of logging trucks twenty thousand miles long—that's how much timber is taken out of our Northwest forests each year."

Like their Canadian counterparts, many American foresters and forestry workers are disturbed by what they see happening to public woodlands. Jeff DeBonis, a National Forest Service Timber Sale Planner, expressed his frustration and alarm in an open letter to his boss, the U.S. Forest Service Chief: "Our basic problem is that we [the Forest Service] are much too biased towards the resource-extraction industries, particularly to the timber industry.... We are overcutting our National Forests at the expense of other resource values. We are incurring negative, cumulative impacts to our watershed, fisheries, wildlife and other non-commodity resources in our quest to meet our timber targets."

For the most part, disposable diapers and women's sanitary products aren't fabricated out of magnificent giants yanked from old growth forests, thank heaven. But that's about all that can be said. The wood which yields the "fluff pulp" for these disposables hails from "fiber farms" or "tree planta-tions," located mainly in the southern United States, and these operations have their own serious shortcomings. Forest ecologist Chris Maser of Corvallis, Oregon, points out that North Americans are making the true forest extinct by grow-ing trees as a "crop." "What we're trading our forests in on are very simplified plantations, and so far as I'm aware, no plan-tation...has been sustainable beyond three short rotations." If plantations really *are* necessary, surely the paper products they yield could at least boast a longer lifetime than a diaper and, better still, be fully recyclable.

The business of making pulp and paper products is huge— and hugely profitable—in North America. Canada is the world's largest exporter of pulp and paper. Add solid wood commodities like plywood, shakes and shingles, and endless stacks of two-by-fours to the annual tonnage of pulp and paper products, and the Canadian forest products industry rings up sales of about thirty billion dollars every year. Well over half of these pulp, paper and wood products leave the country for markets south of the border or offshore while most of the pollutants stay home.

The United States, meanwhile, grosses about two hundred billion dollars annually in sales—"the largest producer and consumer of paper and allied products in the entire world," exults the American Paper Institute. Led by two giants— International Paper and Georgia Pacific—several pulp and paper companies rank high every year on the Fortune 500 list of top American corporations. Sales for these two companies, *despite* a glut of paper, totalled more than twenty-five billion dollars in 1990, more than the GNP of many developing countries.

With numbers like this, why do pulp and paper company executives so often cry poor when pressed for environmental improvements? Part of the answer is that, despite impressive profits many years, there are periodic slumps which are, in fact, occasionally quite abysmal. (For example: "Forest industry tumbles into red. Losses could reach $2-billion for 1991, Price Waterhouse says," a headline about the Canadian forestry sector that appeared in the Toronto *Globe and Mail* in late September, 1991.) While the industry was in the second year of a cyclic slump in mid-1991 when we wrote this book, profits were nothing less than spectacular during the preceding boom years, 1985 to 1989. Even during these good years, however, the amount spent on environmental projects was dwarfed by capital improvements and expansions.

The sheer volume produced by the scores of pulp mills on both sides of the border is breathtaking. For example, the Northwood Pulp and Timber mill in Prince George, British Columbia, churns out fifteen hundred metric tons of bleached kraft pulp *every day*. That's more than half a million tons per year—quite typical for this type of mill. The North

American industry as a whole converts enormous quantities of wood fiber into twelve thousand different kinds of pulp, paper and paperboard products. Rayon and cellophane, printing and writing papers, fluff pulp (for diapers and sanitary napkins), tissue and toilet paper, corrugated cardboard and brown kraft wrapping paper are just part of this lineup.

How a large, round and very solid raw log gets transformed into a sanitary napkin, as well as all manner of other paper products, is a fascinating process. We'll describe, very briefly, how the industry's two major pulp manufacturing processes work. Knowing the differences can help you make better "green" choices among the products they yield.

Let it first be said that, aside from organochlorines, all pulping processes are extremely dirty unless the mill takes proper pollution abatement steps. If not filtered out, leftover shreds of wood fiber, bark and other organic material can settle by the ton to the floor of lakes and rivers, making them uninhabitable for bottom dwellers. What's more, as these mill discharges decay, they can rob the surrounding water of oxygen, causing fish and other aquatic life to suffocate. And pulping leftovers like tree resins and fatty acids are also poisonous to fish.

A word about the composition of wood, the raw material. About 50 percent of wood consists of *cellulose*, which is a tough, fibrous, white material and the crucial ingredient in all paper products. In raw wood, the cellulose is "glued" together by *lignin*, which makes up another 30 percent of the total wood mass. *Aromatic oils* and *resins* account for most of the remainder. The tough cellulose fibers in wood have to be made into soft, crumbly pulps before they can be converted into any of the twelve thousand different end products.

One method is *mechanical pulping*. In the mechanical process, raw wood is literally ground to a pulp. This is the most efficient way to use raw logs—about 95 percent of the wood, including most of the lignin, ends up transformed into usable pulp. From an environmental standpoint, this is the first big plus for mechanical pulping—very little of the tree is wasted.

Mechanically grinding raw wood does takes its toll on the cellulose by chopping it into relatively short fibers. Most mechanical pulp is made into newsprint which, as you're aware, is fairly flimsy paper, with little "tear strength."

In some cases, mechanical pulps are treated with steam heat and sulfur-based chemicals in a process called Chemi-Thermo-Mechanical Pulping or CTMP. This treatment removes some of the lignin and resin from the wood, resulting in a stronger, lighter, more absorbent pulp than groundwood that can be used for sanitary napkins and disposable diapers.

Another environmentally desirable characteristic of mechanical pulps is that they're brightened—not bleached in the true sense of the word—to a cream color with hydrogen peroxide. They are *not* treated with any chlorine bleaching agents. Hydrogen peroxide is probably the most environmentally friendly chemical used in the pulp and paper industry because it breaks down into two familiar substances, oxygen and water. In the brightening process, it transforms leftover lignin in the pulp to a lighter color, but doesn't actually remove it. (In direct sunlight, this lignin reverts back to its natural yellowish-brown practically before your eyes. A newspaper left out in the sun for a few hours is proof positive of this phenomenon, called "brightness reversion.")

The other major pulping process—and it accounts for the lion's share of all pulps made in North America—is *chemical pulping*. There are two main types: the *kraft* (also called *sulfate*) process, which predominates, and *sulfite* pulping. Your nose recognizes chemical pulps instantly, distinguished as they are by an unforgettable rotten-egg odor that drifts with the breezes around mill sites.

Kraft fibers are renowned for their length and strength. In fact, its name is the German word for strong. But only about half the raw wood—just the cellulose—ends up in finished kraft pulp. Nearly all of the remaining material is literally cooked out using caustic chemicals. These leftover wood wastes are usually captured and then burned for fuel, making this process energy self-sufficient. Unbleached kraft pulp is medium brown in color because of the unwanted lignins, resins and tree oils that stay in the pulp. Although only 6 to 10 percent of this material remains after cooking with caustic soda, it's enough to keep the pulp "paper bag" brown.

To produce the most prized and lucrative type of kraft— the bright white variety—mills move the unbleached pulp through a subsequent bleaching sequence. This process—a series of steps, really—is the source of kraft's batch of toxic organochlorines, which are mainly produced when chlorine gas is applied to dissolve what's left of the brownish-colored lignin out of the cellulose fibers.

Replacing pure chlorine with chlorine dioxide, as explained in Chapter 1, helps decrease the total organochlorine output. And there are two other ways to tackle the problem if chlorine-based bleaching agents are used: by pre-treating the pulp using oxygen, which unfortunately also tends to attack the cellulose fibers if applied for too long. Oxygen *can* totally replace the chlorine if we settle for a pulp that's not "whiter than white," an option certainly worth considering. Another way to lessen the formation of organochlorines is by using a stage called *extended delignification*, where the pulp is cooked longer in caustic soda. Yet even these measures do not totally eliminate the organochlorine by-products.

The second chemical pulping process, called *sulfite* pulping, produces a pulp that is lighter in color than kraft, because it contains less lignin, but it is also weaker and softer. Chlorine bleaching compounds are then used to achieve bright whiteness (along with the inevitable toxic discharges). Given its softness, sulfite pulp is often used to make tissue products like paper towels and toilet paper.

North American disposable diapers, women's sanitary napkins and incontinence pads are made from "fluff" pulp, which is just as it sounds, fleecy and absorbent. All three pulps we've described, the CTMP mechanical pulp and the two chemical pulps, kraft and sulfite, can be transformed into fluff. What is the pulp of choice? None other than "whiter-than-white" bleached kraft, which accounts for about 80 percent of these products. This kraft fluff is very absorbent with excellent "mat integrity," which means it doesn't fall apart readily.

Given chlorine-bleached fluff's environmental sins, are there any better alternatives? We wish there were simple answers. Yes, there are disposable sanitary napkins and diapers now on the market made from CTMP, the cream-colored mechanical pulp that isn't bleached with any chlorine-based agents and uses only about half the trees required to make the same amount of kraft pulp. But, despite being chlorine-free, the effluent from CTMP pulp is still quite difficult to render non-toxic. The best option would be sanitary products using CTMP fluff purchased from a totally "closed-loop" mill (one which recycles its process water and chemicals and discharges almost no pollutants), but this is still pie-in-the-sky, since the only closed-loop CTMP mill we know of, Millar Western in northern Saskatchewan, will be making printing papers, not fluff pulp, when it starts producing in March, 1992.

Another excellent bet would be sanitary products made from totally chlorine-free kraft fluff, but nothing yet in North America. However, there's reason to hope: in late 1991, Howe Sound Pulp & Paper Ltd. of Port Mellon, British Columbia, began churning out this continent's first chlorine-free softwood kraft pulp. Like Millar Western's closed-loop CTMP, this pulp is also destined to become printing paper, but with enough pressure on sanitary product manufacturers, surely some of this production can be converted to fluff.

And still another good choice would be to use sulfite fluff made without any chlorine compounds. At least one mill in Canada has switched to chlorine-free pulping for tissue products, Stora's Port Hawkesbury, Nova Scotia, plant, but—this is beginning to sound like a broken record—it's not being converted to fluff pulp suitable for sanitary products yet. (Unfortunately, another sulfite pulpmaker, Fraser Company's Atholville mill in New Brunswick, switched over to chlorine-free in 1990, then shut down in late 1991, at least for a year and perhaps for good, management said.)

The few sanitary products made from cream-colored CTMP fluff have reportedly had problems with "mat integrity" because CTMP's cellulose fibers are shorter than kraft's, and their absorbency is not as great. These problems are being successfully addressed, according to one Quebec-based CTMP manufacturer. (The question is: how much integrity is needed for a single-use disposable product? And another question, even more important: Do we even need them at all? But that's for a later chapter.)

The brand name sanitary protection companies don't even offer CTMP or totally chlorine compound-free products yet. A small handful of CTMP pads and diapers are available as house brands at some supermarket and pharmacy chains, as well as by catalogue from environment friendly mail-order companies. But they're few and far between.

Part of the problem may be that the concept of "chlorine free" is relatively new to North Americans. It's really a European import. We're still struggling with environmental concepts like "non-de-inked paper" and "100 percent recycled from post-consumer waste."

But, in our opinion, a bigger problem is that there are so many mixed messages about chlorine. It's very difficult for anybody, let alone the average consumer, to sort out fact from fiction. The North American industry surely must want us to stay confused. Most pulp companies have just spent, or are in the process of spending, millions of dollars trying to fix up the old chlorine gas process—so they can continue to put out white bleached pulp. At the same time, they're trying to convince us that any problems with dioxins, furans and all those other organochlorines are long gone. A few mills are hedging their bets. They run totally chlorine-free pulps for European customers between batches of conventional bleached kraft, trying desperately to keep customers on both sides of the Atlantic happy. "The market will decide," pulp and paper executives maintain as they sit—rather nervously, we think—on the fence.

The authors of a comprehensive report on the bleached kraft pulp industry in Ontario prepared for the province's environment ministry, come to an interesting conclusion with respect to whiteness while conceding there's still much that's a mystery in the effluent: "The particular organochlorine compounds making up the bulk of the organochlorines in a given effluent are not yet known, will probably never be completely known, and in any case will vary over time. However, it is assumed that a reduction in total chlorinated organics will proportionately reduce the dangerous ones, and that is the approach recommended here. *Obviously the safest procedure would be total elimination of organochlorines from all discharges. This seems unrealistic at present if we continue to demand high brightness white paper* (emphasis ours)."

The question is: who is demanding whiter-than-white paper? Not ordinary consumers, who have overwhelmingly said they're ready and willing to buy and use unbleached or less-bleached products when they're available. (More than 90 percent said "yes" on a recent Angus Reid poll in Canada, and this support has held up over several surveys.) We especially don't need chlorine-bleached sanitary products and disposable diapers. They're not sterile, so why should they be dazzlingly white? We're sure that the marketing wizards who made "whiter than white" a household phrase can also do wonders for "beautiful beige, the better alternative."

Meanwhile, the consumer market is still waiting—to this point in vain—for a whole range of environmentally safe paper products made from unbleached and chlorine-free pulps, recycled wherever possible.

We could wait a long time. Let's demand a choice, and then indeed, "Let the market decide!"

3
Sanitary napkins:
Padding the bottom line

As women, we're big consumers of one category in particular of pulp and paper merchandise—the so-called sanitary protection or feminine hygiene products. We *are* the market for tampons, sanitary napkins and panty liners. We buy them by the billions every year.

And talk about a captive market. Our biological fate is to menstruate nearly a week per month for about half of our lives. A total of eighty-five million Canadian and American women currently fall into the average menstrual age range, from about twelve to fifty years. We've been thoroughly conditioned to using disposable sanitary products. And we rarely discuss them. Add it all up and it's no wonder manufacturers are confident about the steady market for their merchandise, even in recessionary times. "The demand for Tampax products is not affected by the vicissitudes of the economy," proclaimed the 1990 Tambrands Inc. annual report, in what surely must have been the understatement of the year.

Until the 1920s, women used washable bandages or "diapers" made from materials with quaint-sounding names such as "bird's-eye" and "outing flannel" for sanitary protection. Bulky and uncomfortable, these homemade menstrual pads weren't much of an improvement over the basic bandage used many centuries earlier by women of the Roman Empire, or the grass and vegetable fiber contrivances made by women in Australia and Africa.

After a failed attempt by Johnson & Johnson to market a disposable sanitary napkin in the late 1890s—the moral climate of the day ruled out advertising—French nurses experimented during the First World War with cellulose surgical gauze and discovered it made an efficient, comfortable menstrual pad. In 1921, the Cellucotton Products Company—now Kimberly-Clark Corporation—marketed the first disposable in the United States under the trade name Kotex.

And the rest is history, a true rags to riches story, if you'll forgive the pun. Today, North American women spend close to two billion dollars a year on disposable pads and tampons. French nurses may have started the trend seventy-five years ago, but multinationals control nearly all of the action now.

Fortune 500 companies Procter & Gamble, Johnson & Johnson, Kimberly-Clark and Tambrands have a complete stranglehold on the menstrual products market. And men virtually run the whole show. Scanning the 1990 annual reports of these four U.S.-based corporations, we found only one woman in upper management who was well-placed to influence key product and marketing decisions.

About 1.3 billion sanitary pads were landfilled or incinerated in Canada in 1990. In the United States, the figure is even more staggering—11.3 billion. A woman throws away ten thousand pads or tampons in her lifetime, quite a bundle if you had to dispose of them all in your own backyard. Women rarely talk about these disposable, single-use products, but it's past time we had a closer look at them, especially their environmental implications. (There are so many issues with tampons, they receive not one but two chapters of their own. See Chapters 5 and 6.)

Menstrual pads aren't complicated products. There's an absorbent, cotton-like core made from wood pulp, a plastic, moisture-proof liner on the bottom to prevent accidental staining and a softer material, usually rayon or cotton, sheathing the product. Wet-strength agents that keep the pad from falling apart when holding menstrual fluid and surfactants to improve absorbency may also be part of the manufacturer's formula. Glue holds all of these "ingredients" together.

Slim "maxi" products such as Johnson & Johnson's Sure & Natural and P&G's Always Ultra include another component. Both are impregnated with synthetic gelling crystals that can absorb many times their weight in liquids. The safety of these super-absorbent polyacrylates was hotly debated when companies began using them in ultra-thin disposable diapers in 1986, but their presence in sanitary pads is almost unknown and is rarely questioned.

In the United States, the ingredients in "beauty products" such as shampoo and nail polish, as well as a host of other items far less intimate than feminine hygiene products, must be fully listed on their packaging. But this is not a legal requirement for menstrual pads or tampons in either Canada or the U. S., and the companies don't disclose their contents voluntarily.

Despite the competitive nature of the sanitary protection market, with a few major manufacturers and a handful of independents scrapping for a relatively fixed number of consumers, sanitary napkins didn't change much in the fifty years after the first Kotex pads hit the shelves in 1921. The first major innovation appeared in 1970 when Johnson & Johnson introduced its Stayfree mini-pad, a beltless product with a self-adhesive strip down the middle. Beltless pads are now the standard.

Since the number of menstruating women in North America is apparently growing by a meager 1 percent per year, manufacturers are always looking for new ways to increase sales. One is through aggressive expansion into "underdeveloped" markets for disposable sanitary products, such as Eastern Europe, the Soviet Union and the Pacific Rim.

But the industry has also managed to convince North American women we need even more "protection." Marketing data indicate that demand for externally worn sanitary products has climbed in recent years by about 5 percent annually, much higher than the increase in total customers. Yet how can we possibly need more protection for a biological function limited to a few days per month? What's the trick?

Enter the panty liner. This thin pad with the non-biodegradable backing has captured a third of all sanitary napkin sales. Initially designed to help women through the waning days of their periods or to supplement a tampon, panty liners are now being advertised as an essential part of a woman's hygiene *every* day, all month long. "To keep you feeling clean and fresh every day. As part of daily hygiene," says the package of Johnson & Johnson's Carefree deodorant panty shields. Procter & Gamble's booklet, "Periods and Puberty: a practical guide for girls," tells teenagers that its Always panty liner is "great for very light flow days (like the last day of your period or between periods to absorb vaginal discharge). Many teens also like to wear pantiliners right before their periods are due, so they won't be caught by surprise."

And we've bought their ploy, hook, line and sinker. Sad to say, this sort of "information" feeds the notion that women are in a perpetual state of uncleanliness. Some vaginal discharge is natural between periods, but unless a woman is suffering from an infection, she should never produce a discharge heavy enough to warrant a panty liner, even when pregnant. The everyday panty liner ranks right up there with deodorized sanitary pads, vaginal sprays and douches as unnecessary products devised by companies hungry to boost their sales.

The authors of *The Curse: A Cultural History of Menstruation* say that sanitary protection companies go to great lengths to push their wares. "Manufacturers have relied heavily on gimmickry to liven up sales. The huge success of vaginal deodorant sales (the manufacturers first created the need and then rushed to fill it) inspired napkin and tampon makers to capitalize on the odor mania and 'deodorize' their products. What passes for deodorant in most napkins is, of course, perfume."

In the United States, menstrual pads are considered "medical devices" and so are subject to government regulation. Scented or deodorized pads are deemed medium-risk medical devices because of government concerns about the safety of fragrance additives used by manufacturers, and sanitary protection companies are subject to the American government's Good Manufacturing Practices Code. The Food and Drug Administration is required to inspect their facilities every two years.

In Canada, tongue depressors, bandages and dental floss are considered medical devices, but not women's menstrual pads. Interesting. Sanitary products can be placed on the market without prior evidence of safety or efficacy. Testing or monitoring of these products before they're sold in Canada is done entirely at the discretion of manufacturers, mostly for the purpose of quality control. Worse, there are no formal mechanisms in place for monitoring negative health effects once they're on the market.

When it comes to environmental friendliness, sanitary napkins are real losers. Pulping processes dump tons of organochlorines into the atmosphere and waterways, they're overpackaged and impregnated with plastic and they get discarded by the billions into incinerators and landfili sites.

Nearly all disposable sanitary products on the North American market are made from chlorine gas or chlorine-dioxide bleached kraft pulps. When Greenpeace released confidential paper industry documents in 1987 showing that traces of the most toxic dioxins and furans were present in everyday paper products, the media was soon hot on the story's trail. The Canadian Broadcasting Corporation's television program *Marketplace* asked analytical chemist Thomas Tiernan of Wright State University in Dayton, Ohio, to conduct independent tests. He found 2,3,7,8-TCDD (the most potent dioxin) in facial tissues, paper plates and paper towels, and 2,3,7,8-TCDF (the most potent furan) in women's sanitary pads, disposable baby diapers and coffee filters.

The American pulp and paper industry has sponsored risk assessments of the dioxins and furans in these products and assure us they are safe. The U.S. Environmental Protection Agency has also concluded that trace levels of dioxin are "no cause for alarm," a verdict echoed by Canada's Department of Health and Welfare.

In our opinion, industry risk assessments aren't necessarily reassuring. Their conclusions are based more on assumptions and speculation than on concrete data. "Safe levels" of dioxin (and its toxic equivalents) were calculated to be 2.5 times higher in sanitary napkins than in toilet paper. This is a puzzling result. Women who use pads are exposed to the products for hours and even days, compared to an exposure time measured in seconds for toilet paper. An additional note: calculations for disposable diapers included a special correction factor for babies' sensitive skin. No such special consideration for women!

Nowhere in any of these product risk assessments, of course, is there any mention of the impact of manufacturing these chlorine-bleached products on the environment around pulp mills. And nowhere is there any mention of all those other organochlorines about which science still knows so very little.

George Petty, past chairman of the Canadian Pulp and Paper Association, is not known for mincing words. Here's how he dismissed concerns in 1989 about toxic organochlorines: "Dioxins are a non-issue. A baby would have to eat seven thousand diapers a day to get sick from dioxin, never mind wear them. What [environmentalists] managed to do in Europe is to get people paranoid about using white paper, not on any factual analysis, but on scare tactics. I think it is important that we as an industry don't let the Europeans show us this kind of leadership in this country."

Frankly, the kind of leadership *we'd* like to see in North America is one that doesn't descend to silly arguments about "eating diapers" to defend unnecessary bleaching of paper products with chlorine compounds to make them bright white.

What happened in the wake of the "dioxin-in-paper" scare in 1987? Did the market abandon chlorine-bleached products in favor of more environmentally benign alternatives? In Sweden, government officials reacted emphatically to reports about organochlorines in paper products. In June, 1988, Environment Minister Brigitta Dahl stated: "Consumers will not be required to live with an environmental threat on their breakfast tables, in their bathrooms and in large parts of their everyday lives…. If we get chlorine-bleached paper out of consumer products, we will also lose huge amounts of chlorine from the industrial process."

In Europe generally, the discovery of dioxins and furans in paper products sparked off a debate over product safety, but the issue rapidly escalated to encompass the broader environmental concerns associated with chlorine-bleached paper products. "Today, the stronger focus is on the production of pulp mill discharges," says Eva Smith, the Deputy Assistant Undersecretary of the Swedish Ministry of the Environment. "Before buying white paper products, many consumers in Europe want to know how the pulp is produced and the amount of organochlorines going into the environment from the bleaching process."

To satisfy the growing demand for less chlorine, retailers and environmental organizations in Europe have created classification schemes that rank household paper products for "environmental friendliness." A product's rating depends on whether it is recycled, bleached or unbleached. Bleached products are further classified as chlorine-free, low-chlorine, or conventional chlorine, and the rating depends on the amount of chlorine-based compounds leaving the paper mill per ton of pulp. Manufacturers of paper products must submit detailed information about mill discharges and processes to earn the appropriate logo. Sweden's Nature Conservancy sponsors one such ranking program. According to Eva Smith, manufacturers are eager to acquire the chlorine-free logo for their products. To earn this rating, mill effluents must not exceed 0.1 kilograms of AOX per metric ton of paper product.

Greenpeace's Renate Kroesa confirms that chlorine-free sanitary napkins are available in limited quantities in Europe and Australia, but unfortunately the short supply of appropriate pulp—the chlorine-free CTMP for instance—is hindering widespread availability of these products.

The contrast between North America and Europe is striking—the market here has barely budged. Very few sanitary napkins carry "chlorine-free" labels on their product boxes. Nearly all are still whitened and brightened with chlorine gas or chlorine dioxide.

Loblaws, the Canadian supermarket chain that's cashing in on the popularity of "green" products, launched an unscented, chlorine-free sanitary pad in 1990. The packaging states clearly, "It's no longer necessary to produce sanitary napkins using chlorine-bleached fluff pulp." This Loblaws' product is made from mechanical pulp lightened to a cream color with hydrogen peroxide bleach. The A & P food chain offers a similar house brand in Canada.

There are a few other chlorine-free sanitary napkins on the shelves, but they're mostly found in smaller retail outlets like health food stores. They're also available by catalogue from Seventh Generation in Vermont and Natural Order in Toronto, made from chlorine-free mechanical pulp. But not one of the major manufacturers—Tambrands, Procter & Gamble, Johnson & Johnson or Kimberly-Clark—has taken the big step—dispensing with all chlorine agents in any North American sanitary napkin brand.

Here's a rundown of the pulp used by the major corporations in North American sanitary napkins:

- Tambrands says it uses bleached kraft pulp in its Maxithin pads but claims that the pulp suppliers have modified their processes to minimize the production of organochlorine compounds. Some chlorine gas is still used, but the company reports that Tambrands products have been tested for dioxins and furans and "they have been found to be safe."
- Johnson & Johnson's public affairs representatives in Montreal would not confirm the bleaching process used in their Stayfree and Carefree products, but a "consumer consultant" answering questions on the company's toll-free telephone line said the pulp was still bleached with chlorine gas. Interestingly, Johnson & Johnson's sister company

in Britain uses "non-chlorine bleached" pulp in its two brands of sanitary napkins—Vespre and Vespre Silhouette.

- Kimberly-Clark's environmental representatives in Toronto refused to give us any specifics about the pulping processes used in their North American mills. In Britain, K-C's line is called Simplicity and the words "environmentally-friendly pulp" are flashed across the front of the package. The Women's Environmental Network in London received assurances that Kimberly-Clark's pads are not chlorine-bleached and contain no optical brightening agents. But do these words mean that no chlorine-dioxide is used? The answer is not clear.

- The fluff pulp for Procter & Gamble's Always brand comes from the company's mill in Foley, Florida. P&G spokesperson Dennis Darby says the company has eliminated chlorine gas in the bleaching process and now relies solely on chlorine dioxide. Other process changes have resulted in the reduction of mill discharges to 0.9 kilograms AOX per ton of dried pulp. Compared to the other big North American "name" brands, this AOX level is excellent. Under a European rating system such as the Swedish Nature Conservancy's, however, paper products made with Foley pulp would not earn even a "low-chlorine" grade. To achieve that rating, organochlorine discharges would still have to be cut in half.

Bright white products, of course, create the impression of hygiene and cleanliness. But consumers should know that whiteness does not equal sterility—neither sanitary pads nor tampons are sterile products. Nor is "whiteness" or "brightness" usually necessary for the paper product to function better. Removing some of the lignins and resins *is* required if the pulp is being used for sanitary products like facial tissue, toilet paper and menstrual pads—the pulp becomes more absorbent. It is not essential, however, to bleach pulp to a very high brightness to achieve adequate absorbency. And treating pulp with chlorine-based chemicals isn't the only answer. Renate Kroesa of Greenpeace says hydrogen peroxide effectively removes the resin acids without the negative side effects of chlorine bleaching. She points out that fluffing and special drying techniques can also increase the absorption potential of pulp.

Interesting to note, Melitta Inc., the coffee filter manufacturer, has recently introduced a new product line made from unbleached brown kraft pulp. Absorbency is a critical factor in coffee filters, just as it is in sanitary napkins. Company spokesperson Joda Hoffman says the new unbleached product performs as well as the original "white" filter. Melitta achieved satisfactory absorbency by putting the unbleached paper through a special crimping process that enhances its ability to absorb liquids at the appropriate rate.

Sulfite pulp is another alternative to chlorine-bleached kraft pulp for sanitary products. Sulfite comes out of the pulping process a creamy beige color which can be lightened satisfactorily with hydrogen peroxide and oxygen. This pulp is softer and weaker than kraft, but strength is not critical for sanitary and tissue products.

The continued use of chlorine-bleached pulp is a sign that environmental concerns are not high on the list of priorities of North American sanitary protection companies. Nor has disposability made much of an impression. Walk down the aisle of any supermarket or drugstore and survey the sizeable sanitary products section for a moment. You'd never know we have a serious solid waste disposal problem on our hands.

Environmentalist Marjorie Lamb says in her book, *Two Minutes a Day for a Greener Planet*, that aside from chlorine bleaching, her major complaint with sanitary products is "the excessive and unnecessary use of plastics, which never break down in the environment." And there are plastics both inside and out. Synthetics and plastics are part and parcel of the napkins themselves, virtually nullifying their already slim chances of breaking down in a landfill site. The bottom liner is made of non-biodegradable polypropylene, and the soft, non-woven coverings may also be plastic—Procter & Gamble's Always pad, for example, uses a "breathable" polyethylene. Other producers have opted for materials such as woven rayon, polyester and cotton, each having its own environmental drawbacks.

Let's not forget there's still more plastic on the outside. It's called "polybagging," the latest trend in product packaging, which has overtaken cardboard. Not one of these thick outer wraps mentions any recycled content. (Most of these purchases are probably bagged yet again in plastic at the checkout counter, for "discretion's sake.") A few brands, including Tambrands' Maxithins and Johnson & Johnson's Stayfree and Sure & Natural Prima, are still boxed in cardboard but, as of this writing, only Johnson & Johnson stated that their cartons were made from 100 percent recycled paper.

The advent of individually wrapped sanitary pads is another product "innovation" that thumbs its nose at the solid waste crisis, a case of overpackaging gone mad. An industry trade journal says individual wrapping—even though the product is not sterile—has been a boon to the major brands and the private label manufacturers who claim that "today's consumer is more active and therefore more concerned about discretion."

Industry analyst Bonita Austin of Wertheim Schroder & Co. in New York believes that environmental considerations don't figure prominently when a woman is purchasing sanitary products. Tambrands Canada agrees. A company spokesperson told us that while a lot of women are concerned about the environment, the "number one consideration is whether a product meets their needs."

How about meeting our needs *and* striving to satisfy environmental concerns?

The recent launch of Johnson & Johnson's new Sure & Natural Prima pad should have made much of its environmental benefits, at least compared to other sanitary products. This maxi pad is as thin as a panty liner and has a brown-colored absorbent core made of sphagnum moss, the water-absorbent plant found abundantly in wetland bogs. But this product was launched in Canada with no mention at all of its earthly origins. The package leaflet says only that the pad's absorbent power comes from a "unique, highly absorbent core from nature that draws in fluid so well, the napkin doesn't need to be thick."

When pressed, company executives did emphasize the product's positive environmental features, and later mounted a TV ad campaign portraying a young woman cooing over sphagnum moss in a tranquil forest setting. Dr. Patricia Ramicieri, director of Johnson & Johnson's product development research laboratory in Montreal, stressed that the core is natural, and that "we don't use any harsh chemicals to process the sphagnum. No bleaching." She also pointed out that the slimness of the product means the amount of waste going to landfills is reduced.

Some environmentalists cautiously welcomed this new product because of its waste reduction potential, but others weren't so sure. Aside from the absorbent core, the pad is still made with a synthetic covering, uses chlorine-bleached pulp and has an expanded, non-biodegradable plastic backing.

Anne Champagne, staff environmentalist with the Federation of Ontario Naturalists, points out that wetlands across Canada are already besieged by development, dredging and agriculture. Johnson & Johnson counters that 12 percent of Canada is covered with sphagnum moss, and that the company will never use more than 1 percent of the new annual growth. (Let's get that promise in writing from *all* the sanitary protection companies.)

It's obvious that women who are concerned about the environmental impact of their use and disposal of sanitary protection products are faced with a dilemma. We're offered more and more plastic wrapping, and still more plastic, in the name of feminine discretion. We're being kept in the dark about organochlorine discharges from the production of wood pulps used in the products even as they're unnecessarily bleached to a bright white.

We find the total lack of "environmentally friendly" options offered by brand-name manufacturers unacceptable. Why aren't producers moving to incorporate recycled pulp in all of their packaging? Why aren't they eliminating petroleum-dependent plastic rather than rushing to it ever more enthusiastically? Or—most important—why aren't they cutting out chlorine gas and all related compounds—chlorine dioxide and hypochlorite—in the bleaching of pulp used for feminine hygiene products? As we were finishing this book, one private-label manufacturer told us that other major pulp producers were following Procter & Gamble's lead by planning to introduce low chlorine fluff. Even if this is true, we say "get the chlorine out" altogether. We can cope with off-white sanitary pads. We also think most women using disposables would be willing to settle for a little less "performance" in their sanitary pad as an inconsequential trade-off for a cleaner environment. (Still, women shouldn't have to settle for less. Surely if manufacturers put their minds to it, they can develop a chlorine-free product which matches the quality of their "whiter-than-white" pads. If they can put a man on the moon...)

We also find the industry far more secretive and proprietary than it needs to be. Far too often our questions were answered with silence, and sometimes as if we had no damn business asking. One Kimberly-Clark employee in Toronto curtly sidestepped our queries about environmental issues: "When we're ready to share things with the public, we'll do that," he said. That kind of paternalistic attitude we definitely don't need.

So far, it seems that most of the North American sanitary protection industry is immune to the new environmental ethos. But in our opinion—and a growing number of women agree—there's no reason why we should put aside our environmental concerns when we make decisions about sanitary products. Disposable products should only be used sensibly and sparingly. If sanitary protection companies are not going to provide us with more environmentally sound options, there are alternatives.

4
Disposable diapers:
A rash of misinformation

Over the past few years, with landfill sites around North America rapidly filling up to capacity and few alternative sites available, disposable diapers have become the target of increasing condemnation from parents, politicians and environmentalists, all roundly critical of this bulky, throwaway product.

In August, 1990, Procter & Gamble and Kimberly-Clark, North American's two largest producers of "dispo diapers" (as one Greenpeacer calls them), were both slapped with Wastemaker Awards by Wastewatch, an environmental coalition based in Washington, D.C. These awards came just two months after the release of an American Gallup poll that showed a surprising number of consumers—close to half—favor taxing or even banning disposables altogether to protect the environment.

The manufacturers think they're getting—what else?—a bum rap. "We don't really know why disposable diapers became the lightning rod of public sentiment about garbage," said Procter & Gamble's Robert Greene recently in *Advertising Age* magazine. Greene is director of the Paper Section of P & G's Research and Development department, headquartered in Cincinnati. "Even though we're [that is, disposable diapers] only one to two percent of the total solid waste stream, we were singled out as *the* problem."

"Only" 1 or 2 percent translates into a staggering twenty *billion* soggy and soiled plastic-backed disposables making their way into Canadian and American landfill sites every year. Aside from newspapers and beverage and food contain-ers, no other single consumer product adds as much to our bloated solid waste stream.

Still, the disposable diaper will go down in history as one of the greatest success stories in the history of consumerism, dubious as that distinction may be. After a modest start in the 1940s, disposables gathered steam in the 1960s and have steadily eaten into a market once completely "owned" by reusable cloth diapers. They now account for a whopping 85 percent of the total market share. Procter & Gamble main-tains its North American sales are strong, but we're convinced that the tide is turning once again in favor of cloth, at least in Canada, even though definitive market sur-veys are not available (at least not to impecunious book authors unable to afford several thousand dollars for A.C. Nielsen data). International figures, however, continue to skyrocket as Procter & Gamble pushes its disposable diapers into uncharted and, until now, unexploited markets includ-ing South America, Saudi Arabia and the Pacific Rim. P & G's worldwide sales rose a hefty 15 percent in 1990.

Convenience is the big selling point of disposables, and many parents are hooked soon after their baby is born. The addiction begins in the maternity wards of countless hospitals, when nursery staff immediately swaddle newborns in Pampers, Huggies or any one of several competitors. It was once common for diaper companies to make sweet deals with many North American hospitals, but this practice has diminished somewhat. Since the solid waste issue reared its ugly head, hospitals are now thinking more conscientiously about the end result of their great "deals."

But manufacturers still consider new parents fair game. In some hospitals, baby kits that contain free diaper samples and discount coupons are bestowed upon parents when the mother and infant are discharged, and the promotions continue long after their homecoming. The very use of disposables in a hospital implies a medical endorsement of the product that undoubtedly influences new parents—the perception is that hospitals ought to know what's best for newborns.

Even the most ecologically conscious parents can find themselves drawn into the disposable diaper trap. Toronto father Mark Wright described himself as an "environmental hooligan" before the birth of his first child. "I would verbally assault anyone who had the misfortune of buying disposables in my presence," he recounts. But things changed when their own baby was born. Wright was almost as exhausted as his wife Nicole after the delivery and "when the nurse slipped the disposables on our baby, my environmental antennae didn't even twitch."

Cloth diapers were waiting when mother and baby Wil came home, but Wright used the free disposables from the hospital first because he didn't want to "waste" them. Before he knew it, he was running to the store to buy more. "There was no logic in it," he explains. "They just seemed so damned handy."

Wright, by his own admission, was well on his way to becoming a "disposable diaper junkie." His wife finally helped him get a grip on the problem, and now they use cloth diapers full-time. "The interesting thing about this whole issue is that it's a non-issue for me today," Wright says. "Why use a disposable when cloth is as easy? Now that I'm an experienced diaper changer, one's as fast as the other and the convenience factor is no longer part of the argument. Wil has never had any skin problems or rash, so we know cloth is doing its job. Disposables need trees to be produced and landfill to be disposed in—I just see disposable diapers as doing more damage than good."

Parents wouldn't find disposable diapers nearly so convenient if they religiously followed package directions. When disposables are soiled with feces, manufacturers give clear instructions to rinse them in a toilet before they're discarded. How many parents actually do this? Only about 5 percent, according to waste management consultant, Carl Lehrburger. Human waste, and particularly baby stools, carry more than 100 different intestinal viruses, and this waste simply doesn't belong in landfill sites.

It's an expensive venture for parents to stick exclusively with disposables after their newborn arrives home from the hospital. From birth to successful toilet training, they'll pay out more than $2,100 in the name of diapering convenience. This compares to about $1,750 for a diaper service (charges vary from city to city) or, if you decide to wash your own, $200 for the cloth diapers plus the cost of machine washing and drying.

Multiply the costs of disposable diapers by 85 percent of the annual North American birthrate, and you realize that this business is enormously lucrative for manufacturers—it adds up to an astonishing four billion dollars per year. Procter & Gamble and Kimberly-Clark have a stranglehold on this market. They share 80 percent of total sales, with the majority going to P & G and its two brands, Pampers and Luvs.

No wonder these companies are so relentless in their struggle for greater sales; even a marginal loss of market share means millions of dollars shaved off profits. Look around, and you see signs of the battle everywhere. Parents turning on their TV sets are confronted by appeals from "expert" mothers and authoritative pediatricians, all championing the best disposable.

In retail stores, the barrage intensifies—we find superabsorbent diapers, no-frills versions, teddy-bear prints and stretch-waist diapers. Just when we wondered, "What will they think of next?" along came his-and-hers blue and pink diapers with special gender-specific absorbency zones. Then P & G began rolling out its new Phases product, diapers for each stage of infancy. Kimberly-Clark followed quickly with a similar line called Baby Steps. But the biggest potential threat to current sales are consumer worries about the environmental impact of these bulky disposables. A host of new features aim squarely at squelching these concerns—some disposable diapers are now touted as "chemical-free", "biodegradable" or "compostable" (well, *almost* compostable).

First, biodegradable diapers were advocated as a quick-fix solution to the solid waste problem. But environmentalists and the major diaper manufacturers both criticized this innovation. They argued that chances were dismal that these so-called biodegradables would break down any more quickly than regular disposables under all those layers of compacted garbage.

Then Kimberly-Clark and Procter & Gamble stepped into the breach with elaborate plans to recycle and compost diaper products. Kimberly-Clark is currently studying methods to recycle diaper materials into industrial products. The company also claims that several composting studies, including one with the American National Sanitation Foundation, are under way, although company officials were reluctant to provide details.

Recycling diapers requires a series of steps: collection, cleaning, separation and, finally, reprocessing into new materials. In Seattle, Procter & Gamble experimented with separating and recycling the two main ingredients of diapers—plastics and fluff pulp. The corporation envisioned new products such as cardboard boxes and computer paper from the pulp, and flowerpots, garbage bags and "lumber" from the plastics. P & G is sponsoring a feasibility study for a similar project by a Toronto-based company. But the Seattle project has since been wound down. It proved that disposable diapers can be recycled, but the price tag is just too high.

Dennis Darby, a spokesperson with P & G in Toronto, admits that costs are a big obstacle, adding that recycling is very "diaper-specific." "You're only getting at 2 percent of the waste." He's a lot keener on municipal composting, saying enthusiastically that composting could tackle not just the 2 percent of landfill taken up by disposable diapers, but at least half of our garbage problem.

In October, 1990, Procter & Gamble announced a world-wide commitment of twenty-three million dollars to promote municipal composting of garbage. A sizeable chunk of this money is earmarked for grants and technical assistance to communities to encourage them to divert their solid waste from landfills into composting streams.

But there's composting and then there's composting. At its simplest, of course, composting is "cooking" kitchen and garden wastes in backyard and apartment-style containers of various kinds, which in turn yields the nutrient-rich "black gold" so sought after by flower and vegetable gardeners.

At the other end of the spectrum, there's Municipal Solid Waste (MSW) composting, which is exactly the program P & G is trying to promote. As envisioned by Procter & Gamble, MSW composting works like this: all household trash is collected and delivered to a composting facility. After a crude screening of non-compostable materials such as glass, metal and plastic (which are sent away for recycling), the rest is pushed through a series of screens and a metal separator both before and after composting, to sort out undesirable elements.

Some MSW composting systems are already in operation in the United States. One is a private facility in St. Cloud, Minnesota, which includes disposable diapers in its waste stream. In a demonstration project, Procter & Gamble used this facility to see how increasing the load of diapers in the stream would affect compost quality. According to P & G, the results of this experiment were "promising." But for what and whom? A company official later told the Toronto Board of Health that the St. Cloud diaper compost is Grade 1—it can be used in Minnesota for Christmas tree farming, but is not safe for agricultural use.

Similar European facilities have had problems with heavy metals and shards of plastic, glass and grit when they compost the whole waste stream. Concerns about the purity of this compost are echoed in the United States. John Ruston, a waste-disposal specialist with the Environmental Defense Fund explained the difficulties very simply in a recent article in the *New York Times*: "If you try to compost an undifferentiated waste stream, you'll end up mixing batteries with old spaghetti and wind up with contamination."

John Hanson, executive director of the Recycling Council of Ontario, says high-quality compost is essential to the viability of large-scale programs. He favors composting of food and yard wastes, with possibly some low-value paper products such as egg cartons. If municipalities move to large-scale facilities, he'd prefer to see at least a three-stream system. Rather than simply setting out a bag of undifferentiated garbage each week, householders would separate their trash into wet (yard and food wastes), dry (recyclables) and the leftover refuse.

Procter & Gamble came under the gun recently for advertising that promoted diaper composting under the headline: "The new life cycle of a disposable diaper." The series of eight illustrations showed a diaper being miraculously transformed through gradual breakdown from its "just-used" state, finally emerging as a fertile soil conditioner sprouting a healthy young tree seedling. Great idea for the backyard compost heap? Nope. The fine print points out that the diaper is only 80 percent compostable and "must be broken down in the municipal composting system." Twenty percent of the product—the plastic outer cover, tapes and waistband, plus some of the glue and superabsorbent gelling material—simply won't degrade in any accelerated composting system.

Another slight problem: facilities like those in St. Cloud, Minnesota are few and far between. There are none that we know of in Canada. It seems that people have been mislead by this advertisement, including a friend of ours with an MBA. They assume that these composting systems already exist virtually everywhere—and that's what the fine print of this advertisement implies. Outrageous! We discuss the ethical implications of this advertisement more fully in Chapter 7.

Few if any municipalities are even planning composting systems that will welcome diapers. At a recent meeting of recycling coordinators from across Ontario, there was enthusiasm for yard and food composting but according to the Ontario Recycling Council's John Hanson, "The seven who are currently collecting curbside organics all specified that they don't want to compost diapers."

Like many other North American cities, Toronto is considering a composting facility as part of its effort to cut down on solid refuse going to landfill sites. City councillor Elizabeth Amer says that food and organic matter such as kitchen and yard waste would be the first target for a Toronto composting project. She adds, "Anyone who suggests that disposables be composted is missing the point. What we really need to do is reduce consumption."

The makers of disposables fight environmental objections to their products not just in advertising but on other fronts too, including the political one. In 1990, Procter & Gamble launched a major publicity drive to counteract environmental claims about the superiority of cloth diapers and services and to stop governments from passing negative legislation dealing with disposables. Both Procter & Gamble and Kimberly-Clark are using lobbyists, research they claim is independent, and direct mail appeals to persuade people (and politicians) that their disposable products are no worse than the reusable alternatives.

Jeffrey Tryens of the Center for Policy Alternatives in Washington, D.C., has been watching the debate over diapers closely. He thinks Procter & Gamble's strategy is clear. "All they need to do is give parents an 'out' so they'll have an excuse to continue using disposables.... Industry knows that there's a wave of negative public opinion out there and they have to ride it out. Meanwhile, they're showing the public that they're trying to solve the problem, they're creating questions in people's minds about cloth diapers, and they're holding on until concern among the public dies away."

There are pros and cons to all diapering alternatives, P & G contends, a viewpoint clearly intended to alleviate parents' guilt about choosing paper disposables. Deflecting arguments which condemn disposables for their ecological sins, advertising goes on to say that throwaways provide superior dryness and prevent diaper rash better than cloth. To further relieve the environmental stigma of throwaways, Procter & Gamble's brochures emphasize the steps it has taken to decrease the solid waste associated with its disposables. Major reductions *have* been achieved in both the size and bulk of Pampers and its packaging. P & G says the switch from thick to thin "ultra" diapers in 1986 reduced diaper thickness by 50 percent, and reductions in the volume of retail packaging is in the order of 80 percent. These figures apparently hold true for disposables made by other manufacturers as well. All reductions are a step in the right direction, but cutting back the size of individual diapers while producing them in ever-increasing billions around the world is not really saving much where it counts— in trees and at landfill sites.

Many politicians say they've had enough. In the cities of Guelph and Waterloo, Ontario, municipal officials are actively promoting a return to reusable diapers as a way of dealing with their landfill problems. Waterloo's brochure, "Diaper Options," tells parents that cloth diapers are "environmentally preferable," and suggests that disposables should be the exception, not the rule.

By mid-1991, politicians in over twenty U.S. states had tried a variety of tactics to curb disposables. In New Jersey and Colorado, legislative bills were introduced that would require disposable diaper packaging to bear a label describing the "environmental burdens" posed by disposing of the product. Connecticut considered a tax on disposables to encourage the use of cloth alternatives and Vermont's governor proposed a complete ban.

But most of these initiatives failed, died on legislative order papers or were vetoed, testimony to the power of relentless industry lobbying, and no small thanks to a Procter & Gamble-sponsored consultant's report by A.D. Little, which concluded that disposable diapers are no worse for the environment than cloth. This report was cited in a statement by the governor of California vetoing a law that would have required labels on packaging warning consumers about the environmental burdens caused by disposable diapers. The veto finished this bill, of course, but thankfully not all anti-disposable initiatives have failed. As part of an omnibus environmental bill passed in April, 1990, for example, Wisconsin provided sales tax and use-tax exemptions for both reusable cloth diapers and diaper services.

Although disposables are an obvious environmental target, they're actually holding their own and gaining ground in the battle against—diaper rash. Yes, diaper rash has become a key focus in the cloth-versus-disposable "diaper wars" now being waged for the hearts and dollars of consumers across North America. Dr. John Blocker, a pediatrician in Phoenix, Arizona, speaks to us often in magazines and on TV about Pampers' superior ability to keep babies dry. P & G's promotional materials claim modern disposables offer superior skin care conditions that lead to fewer and less severe incidents of diaper rash than cloth.

Meanwhile, cloth fights back. The National Association of Diaper Services in Philadelphia says studies have shown that babies who wear their members' cloth diapers get the dreaded rash five times less often than those who use disposables. "Our research indicates that 54 percent of babies who wear cotton diaper-service diapers never have a rash at all."

So the question again becomes: which source do you believe? Keeping a baby's skin healthy is probably more a product of good diapering practices than whether a parent chooses to use cloth or disposables. It makes sense that diaper rash can be prevented or lessened if babies are changed often and their skin is kept thoroughly clean and free of irritating agents including soap, perfume and so on. Still, the influence of saturation advertising is powerful. Companies like Procter & Gamble have a huge edge in "proving" the superiority of their product against the vagaries of diaper rash.

Superabsorbent "ultra-thin" disposables are another aspect of the issue that deserves closer attention. They landed on store shelves in 1986 and the alarm bells sounded immediately. The superabsorbent agent inside these diapers is crystals made of synthetic polyacrylate. A similar substance had been used in super-absorbency menstrual tampons until 1985, when it was revealed that the material increased the risk of tampon-associated toxic shock syndrome.

Concerns about this material prompted the president of the Empire State Consumer Association, Judy Braiman-Lipson, to petition the U.S. Food and Drug Administration, the New York State attorney general and the Consumer Product Safety Commission to stop the sale of these superabsorbent diapers and adult incontinence pads. The Consumer Product Safety Commission examined the industry's safety data and decided that the polyacrylate granules were safe for infant exposure. Health and Welfare Canada has made a similar pronouncement.

Yet Braiman-Lipson remains unconvinced. She argues that studies simply haven't been done that examine the effects of the polyacrylate granules migrating to the reproductive organs of babies. One mother in Phoenix contacted a local hospital worried about the tiny compressible beads of gel oozing from her four-month-old daughter's vagina. They were found to be the gel matrix from superabsorbent diapers. Manufacturers seem to have a problem creating a "fail-safe" design that keeps the polyacrylate granules inside the diaper linings. Three parents we spoke to had found the round, clear crystals on their babies' skin.

Government standards for infant diapers do not exist in the United States or Canada. This became especially clear after consumer groups raised questions about the superabsorbent diapers. Companies may do their own safety testing before marketing a product but they're not legally required to do so. And they're not required to submit evidence of safety or efficacy before shipping their diapers to the supermarket or pharmacy shelf.

If you're trying to compare the environmental impact of cloth versus disposable diapers, don't look for guidance to the so-called independent life-cycle studies—they're simply misleading. The American National Association of Diaper Services, Procter & Gamble and the diaper manufacturers' arm of the American pulp and paper industry have all sponsored this type of study. Guess which studies favor disposables and which give the nod to cloth? You don't have to be a genius to figure out that only results favorable to the sponsor see the light of day. William Franklin, author of the study financed by the American Paper Institute's Diaper Manufacturers' Group, said as much at a one-day disposable diaper seminar in Toronto—that several of his own client's studies are gathering dust on a shelf because they didn't benefit the sponsor's product or service.

Still, disposable diaper companies are milking the results of favorable life-cycle analyses for all they're worth. Procter & Gamble's "six of one, half a dozen of the other" ad suggests that, environmentally, it's a toss-up between cloth and disposable diapers. While disposable diapers add more garbage to landfills and eat up more raw materials in their manufacture, the ad says, cloth consumes "significantly" more water, energy and fuel, and causes a greater amount of air and water pollution.

The diaper manufacturers' studies pay scant attention to the squandering of raw materials to make disposables, or the consequences of cutting down trees and processing them into pulp fiber. Meanwhile, they exaggerate the impact of cloth diapers by taking into account every conceivable factor, including the energy needed to make the plastic bucket used to hold the soiled diapers! Calculations of energy consumption are another key to the erroneous conclusion that there is no clear environmental winner when cloth and disposables square off. The greatest drain from home laundering is the electricity and gas used to heat the water and run the washer and dryer. The studies assume that home laundering consumes a certain amount of energy, but no one has ever actually examined home laundering practices. The conclusions aren't truly conclusions at all—they're just speculation.

The study by Carl Lehrburger, paid for by the cloth diaper service association, says that diaper services use one-third of the energy required for disposables. Washing reusables at home consumes 60 percent of the energy used for disposables, mostly in the energy-intensive manufacturing process—yet another case where a sponsored study finds results favorable to, yes, the sponsor.

Victoria, B.C., municipal politician Carol Pickup says that any report commissioned by an organization with a vested interest "has no validity." She would like to see an independent body, such as a government agency, do a similar study, unfettered by biases. At its best, an independent "life-cycle" analysis will describe real, verifiable environmental costs associated with the manufacture and use of a product from "cradle to grave." Trouble is, says Hannah Holmes of *Garbage* magazine, who has looked closely at all these analyses, the private sector is the only group with the money to sponsor the studies.

The closest we came to finding objectivity was a scientific critique of two diaper life-cycle studies. Both claimed there is little difference in the environmental impact of cloth versus disposables, and (in case you needed to be told!) both were commissioned by makers of disposables. This critique, prepared for the Women's Environmental Network in Britain by an independent consulting firm, concluded that in the areas of energy use, raw materials, wastewater effluent and domestic solid waste, cloth diapers win by a substantial margin each time.

Canada's federal government obviously agrees, much to the chagrin of disposable diaper manufacturers. By fall, 1991, nine brands of cloth diapers sold in Canada had earned the EcoLogo, the government's stamp of approval for products and services doing the least damage to the environment. Only cloth diapers washed at home and diaper services qualify for the logo. Under the rules, wash-at-home diapers must be made of 100 percent reusable materials and survive at least seventy-five trips through the family washing machine. Environment Canada feels that the environmental benefits of good diaper services actually outperform home-laundering—they conserve resources by using less water, energy and detergent.

Today's disposable diaper is a product of technical and scientific wizardry. Compared to the 100 percent cotton diaper, the disposable of the 1990s is made of a dizzying array of materials, ranging from plastics and synthetics for the outer "shell," inner liner, tapes and tabs, to adhesives, gelling crystals, paper tissue and cotton-like layers of wood pulp.

Eighty percent of a throwaway diaper is made from wood pulp, and almost all of it goes to the absorbent "fluff" core. The number of trees destined to be turned into paper diapers is astonishing—the figure most often quoted comes from the *Financial Times* of London, which says that one *billion* trees are cut down annually to serve this market. That's 4.5 trees per baby.

Forests in Scandinavia and the United States are the major sources of wood fiber for diapers. Procter & Gamble insists that no old-growth forest is cut down to satisfy its need for wood fiber, at least not for its diaper products. "Trees are planted and harvested like a crop, like cotton, in accordance with local environmental regulations," says a P & G promotion piece from Britain. Dennis Darby of Procter & Gamble in Toronto maintains that 50 percent of its wood comes from company-owned tree farms, and the rest from private woodlot owners.

Trees such as spruce and pine grow quickly in the southeastern United States where Procter & Gamble's farms are located. Even Canadian diapers are made from this southern pulp, a surprise to us since Canada is the world's largest exporter of pulp and paper. While tree farming ensures that old-growth forest isn't cut down for the sake of one brief application to a baby's bottom—what an ignominious fate for something as lovely as a tree—monoculture fiber farms have problems of their own.

"Harvesting of these forests entails the removal of all the trees in a given area due to economic expedience," says the Women's Environmental Network in Britain. "However, it has been proven that this practice rapidly exhausts the soil capacity unless inorganic fertilizers are applied. In turn, inorganic fertilizers have been exposed as a severe threat to healthy soil and water ecosystems."

Worse, WEN states, is the impact on biodiversity. "Mono-culture plantations are not 'forests.' They do contain trees, but this is not the sole biological criterion for a forest. Natural forests are diverse and stable, with a variety of tree species of all different ages, living and dead. They are ideal habitats for hundreds, even thousands, of different animals and plants, forming a complex and productive web of associations. Modern forestry…is creating a biodiversity crisis."

Now, about pulp bleaching and all those odious organo-chlorines.

The fluff in most disposable diapers is made from bleached kraft pulp, which uses chlorine-based chemicals as its whitening agent. The remaining disposable diapers on the market are made with Chemi-Thermo-Mechanical Pulp, the chlorine-free process that uses about half the trees required by kraft pulping. Chlorine-free diapers made with CTMP lightened with hydrogen peroxide have been available for several years in Scandinavia and, since early 1989, in Britain under the trade name Peaudouce. CTMP diapers are available in Canada at two supermarket chains, Loblaw's and A&P. In the United States, Seventh Generation offers a chlorine-free product, while the Nappies brand is available through stores such as Stop 'N Shop. Together, however, all chlorine-free diapers comprise only a very small share of the disposable diaper market.

As for dumping organochlorines into our waterways, at least two companies that make kraft fluff for diapers have a much better record than most pulp manufacturers who use chlorine. The reason is simple: they have totally eliminated chlorine gas from their processes. Procter & Gamble and Weyerhaeuser still bleach their pulps with chlorine dioxide, but two preliminary steps discussed in Chapter 2 help reduce its use considerably: 1) extended delignification (the pulp cooks longer than usual in the caustic soda solution to remove lignin), and 2) oxygen delignification, which removes another 50 percent of the unwanted lignin. Only then is the pulp bleached with chlorine dioxide.

The Weyerhaeuser and P & G pulps are similar to the European-style EC (for environmentally compatible) fluff, which means that levels of organochlorines in the water discharges are drastically reduced—to as low as 0.1 kg of AOX per metric ton of pulp in Europe. (Most kraft pulp mills still spew out well over twenty times this level.)

In the final analysis, neither disposable nor cloth diapers are "good" for the environment. The question is, which is less harmful? Groups such as Toronto-based Pollution Probe actively promote a return to reusables but, as researchers for the group point out, they're not so much for cloth as against disposables. Cotton diapers are not environmentally benign. Most of the cotton industry has a lousy track record with pesticides, herbicides and bleaching processes. And after the cotton is fabricated into diapers, they must be laundered using soap, water and power, all of which add their own environmental costs.

But swaddle babies we must, so it makes sense to press the cotton manufacturers for organic, unbleached fiber for reusable diapers, and then get your husband or partner to wash them in environment-friendly soap or detergent and hang them out to dry. Even better, sign up for a diaper service if you can afford one.

As a society we're still hooked on disposable diapers. Some hospitals are making the big switch to cloth, including a coalition of thirteen in the Metro Toronto area alone. But, regrettably, many day-care centers and maternity wards continue to insist on disposables. And even if demand fell immediately by 50 percent, ten billion diapers would still make their way to landfill sites every year.

The pressure to jettison disposables may well intensify when our overburdened dumps are full, and households are forced to pay a stiff penalty for generating extra garbage. This type of surtax is already being levied in some North American cities—Edmonton is one example—where landfill space is rapidly running out. Perhaps that's when Toronto council member Elizabeth Amer's advice about cutting consumption will really hit home, marking the beginning of the end of The Disposable Diaper Era, as the late twentieth century will surely be known to future generations.

It can't possibly end soon enough.

5
Tampons, part one: The big flush

Have you ever flushed one of those plastic tampon applicators, the ones the package says not to flush? Never?

Then who did?

Lying three hundred kilometers (about 180 miles) off the coast of Nova Scotia, tiny Sable Island is home to various species—grey and harbor seals, a variety of seabirds and about two hundred and fifty wild horses. Humans have never really taken to the island, which, buffeted by wind and storm waves in the open sea, is reminiscent of a long and lonely sand dune. Aside from scientists studying the island's flora and fauna and government meteorologists and navigation staff, it's uninhabited by humans.

But other visitors have arrived on Sable Island recently. They're variously known as beach whistles, finger puppets, LPTs (little pink things), torpedos and tube fish. That's right—plastic tampon applicators. Demonstrating remarkable seaworthiness, they're landing on the beach in "significant numbers," according to Zöe Lucas who is studying the invasion of "foreign" plastics on the island.

Most of these applicators probably float out from Halifax, a city that still spews thousands of tons of untreated and unfiltered raw sewage straight into the ocean every year. (On Canada's west coast, the city of Victoria dumps directly into the Pacific, and the Greater Vancouver Regional District grinds up untreated sewage sludge, including tampons and sanitary pads, and pumps it into the Fraser River. Meanwhile, fishermen in Québec behold hundreds of sanitary pads floating downstream out of greater Montreal, which dumps the raw sewage of 1.3 million inhabitants directly into the St. Lawrence River. Awful.)

While the tampons themselves probably sink and slowly degrade, their sturdy plastic sheaths float and, once they hijack ocean currents, can travel long distances. As well as from Halifax, applicators landing on Sable Island might arrive from as far afield as the Florida coast, swept northward on the Gulf Stream. Other possible sources are American cities standing along the eastern seaboard in states such as Massachusetts, New Jersey and New York. These places, as well as other cities across the U.S., have sewage treatment plants, but many of these systems are overloaded and outdated. They can't cope with unexpected floods of storm water, leading to what environmentalists call "the big flush," torrents of raw sewage spilling out into the Atlantic. Plastic tampon applicators in their thousands are a regular feature of these unfortunate overflows.

Cape Cod artist Jay Critchley collects these applicators by the bushel and turns them into highly visible "art" to prod the public conscience. His most pointed message was an applicator sculpture named "Miss Tampon Liberty," a human-sized

replica of America's revered national symbol. Critchley's stat-
ue was fashioned entirely from three thousand plastic "beach
whistles."

Critchley didn't stop there. For three years, he worked
with Massachusetts state representatives to sponsor legislation calling for a ban on the sale of plastic applicators. A
New Jersey group called Clean Ocean Action spearheaded a
similar drive in 1985. Playtex Family Products defended its
plastic applicator in New Jersey, insisting that a ban on this
little implement would deny women consumers freedom of
choice. Instead of changing over to a non-plastic alternative
or getting rid of the applicator altogether, Playtex toyed with
the idea of making an applicator that would sink quickly.

Research into totally dissolvable tampon applicators is the
vogue right now. The question is: will this new generation of
plastics truly biodegrade, and not mimic the so-called
biodegradable garbage bags of yesteryear that shriveled into
tiny pieces but never vanished. More to the point, do we
really need this upcoming version of "little pink things," even
if they will eventually "disappear?" They may be better than
the original LPTs, but not worth the time, trouble or money
to manufacture by the million.

Meanwhile, the flood of traditional plastic applicators continues, joining old pieces of plastic rope, garbage bags,
children's party balloons and polystyrene cups out on the
high seas and eventually, on the beaches. Ishbel Butler of the
Maritime Fishermen's Union Clean Ocean Committee in
Pictou, Nova Scotia, says that plastic items make up more
than one half of all the refuse collected on nearby beaches
these days.

The special characteristics of plastic—its light weight, durability and strength—are worrisome for marine biologists and can be devastating to wildlife. Particles of plastic—and ultimately plastic tampon applicators do break down into small pieces—are eaten by marine life, including seabirds, fish, turtles and whales. At least fifty of the world's two hundred and eighty species of seabirds are known to swallow floating plastic, mistaking it for food such as plankton or fish eggs. Plastics are virtually indigestible and individual pieces can accumulate and lodge in an animal's stomach and intestines, blocking its digestive tract. An estimated two million seabirds and one hundred thousand marine mammals die annually as a direct result of ingesting or being caught in plastic.

Manufacturers say plastic applicators make tampons easier to insert, but talk about overkill for a device that provides fewer than ten seconds of useful service. Right now, *all* plastic applicators are built to last a lifetime. They're made of hardy, long-lasting polyethylene that takes an incredible amount of time to break down in the ocean.

Johnson & Johnson discontinued its plastic applicator product in Britain about six years ago, after a bout of negative publicity. Its applicators continue to wash up on British beaches to this day. And it has been more than ten years since Procter & Gamble took its Rely tampon off the North American market because of its link with toxic shock syndrome, but Stephen Sautner, a researcher with the Clean Ocean Action coalition, says he still occasionally finds one of the oddly shaped plastic Rely applicators on New Jersey's Sandy Hook beach.

Tampon companies blame women for throwing plastics down the toilet, but anti-flush advisories on the outer wrapping are dwarfed by company trade names. For many women, it's obviously a great deal more convenient to do the big flush—out of sight, out of mind—but the applicators inevitably bob up somewhere else, often along the seaboard and far out into the ocean.

In a case of downright hypocrisy, Tambrands—the North American market leader—recently launched its own plastic-sheathed tampon, the Compak, presumably to challenge Playtex's share of this segment of the market. This leap into plastics comes at a time when Tambrands is aggressively promoting the "environmentally friendly" nature of its products. *The Everyday Earthguide*, a free booklet available to Tambrands' product purchasers in 1991, proclaims that the company has been working to make its products more "environmentally sensitive." Mention of the new plastic applicator is conspicuously absent from the *Earthguide*, which instead informs women that eliminating the cellophane overwrap from the Tampax package has reduced waste substantially.

To justify its introduction of Compak, Tambrands claims that some women "like their plastic." A spokesperson in Toronto told us that young, newly menstruating girls find it easier to use the plastic applicator and that "they want it because it's more compact and allows for more discretion." The slogan in television ads for the product proclaims, "Ain't Nobody's Business But Your Own." Tell that to the Sable Island seabirds.

So much for plastic applicators. Now here's something we never knew until visiting a big city sewage treatment facility, this one located in Scarborough, Ontario, east of Toronto. Not only are plastic tampon *applicators* a major headache, but tampons themselves—and even those cardboard applicators—are the devil incarnate for sewage workers. Ever thought about what happens to a tampon once you've flushed it off into the nether regions of your local sewage system? Well, when it finally reaches the treatment plant, it's immediately screened out—along with the plastic applicators, condoms and various other bits of flotsam and jetsam, including goldfish—and trucked off to a sanitary landfill site.

The trouble begins when tampons and similar debris accidentally circumvent the screens and get into the plant's main pipes, pumping machines and sewage digesters. There, they often clog up the works, necessitating difficult and costly repairs, to say nothing of creating a distasteful and sometimes dangerous clean-up job for the unfortunate worker assigned to the task. So, contrary to what the packaging says, don't ever flush any tampon applicator or the tampon itself! Toilet paper only, and never sanitary napkins.

In towns and cities where little or no sewage treatment is available, flushing of tampons and sanitary pads is even more of a no-no. Rivers and oceans are not meant to be even temporary repositories for these used and possibly contaminated items, no matter how biodegradable they're supposed to be. At least for now, the best place for these disposables to end their journey is at a sanitary landfill site.

The present consumer love affair with "natural" products hasn't been lost on tampon companies. Johnson & Johnson's ad for o.b. tampons in the Québec version of *Chatelaine* magazine proclaims they are "*toute naturellement.*" Smith &

Nephew, a private label maker, tells women that its tampon is made "entirely from natural fibres." But "natural" doesn't equal "environment friendly" or free of health risks.

Rayon and cotton are the fibers of choice. Some tampons, especially the "superabsorbent" and "plus" versions are 100 percent rayon, while others are a blend of the two. The closest you'll get to an all-cotton tampon is the Tampax Original Regular in the U.S. and the Tampax Regular in Canada, made of cotton fiber with a viscose rayon overwrap.

Viscose rayon is more absorbent than cotton, mainly because it's made from pure cellulose derived from wood pulp. But this absorbency comes at a huge price. Wood fibers— once "natural"—are subjected to a complex chemical process that involves intensive treatment with chlorine gas and chlorine dioxide. The result, of course, is a slew of organochlorines, including dioxins, being dumped into mill receiving waters, as well as possible contamination of the rayon itself. Rayon producers rank right up there with some of the worst polluters in North America, with three mills in the top five hundred dirtiest industrial companies, according to the National Wildlife Federation.

Tambrands Inc., the American parent company, tries hard to rationalize the need for rayon in its products. One consumer spokesperson, in response to a toll-free telephone call in the U.S., said, "The reason why there are dioxins in tampons is because we use rayon. If we used all cotton, it doesn't absorb as well as rayon. It is not as easy to compress, so you couldn't get the same tampon performance. It would be bigger and more difficult to insert.... It contains little dioxin, not enough to be hazardous to your health. In order to make rayon, wood pulp must be treated with chlorine gas, and dioxin is known to be a by-product of this process. All but a trace amount of dioxin is washed from the fibers."

When we spoke with this woman's supervisor, the Manager of Consumer Services, she downplayed the personal health risks and shifted our attention to alarming environmental concerns associated with rayon production—not a very reassuring tactic. "Because mills are spewing dioxins into the air and water at the site of the mill...they contaminate fish and wildlife, a risk to the river and environment around the mill." Her comments also mentioned the frequently cited red herring that dioxins occur naturally in the environment.

Tambrands Canada buys its fibers from third-party rayon and cotton suppliers and insists that it doesn't have a lot of control over their production processes. However, the company does say that it's pressing suppliers to switch over to new technologies that use less chlorine gas. (Memo to Tambrands: A totally chlorine-compound-free viscose rayon from Scandinavia was released in mid-1991. Details to follow if you wish.)

Numerous everyday paper products such as coffee filters and facial tissues have been tested for organochlorines, but scant attention has been paid to dioxins and furans in women's tampons. Health and Welfare Canada has never bothered to test these products; the Environmental Protection Agency has done some testing and found trace quantities of dioxins; and the Institute of Environmental Chemistry in Sweden detected both dioxins and furans in the parts-per-quadrillion range. Data on the capacity of dioxins, furans and other organochlorines to leach out of paper products and into the human body are sparse generally, and simply don't exist for tampons.

Tambrands Canada assures us that trace levels of dioxins don't pose a health hazard. But not so fast. Despite enormous sums of money spent worldwide on dioxin research, and some studies suggesting there might be a "threshold" or "safe dose" of dioxin below which no toxic effects would occur, the October 18, 1991, edition of *Research News* reports that "the infamous chemical is proving to be even more slippery than many scientists initially suspected." The U.S. Environmental Protection Agency had called for a reevaluation of dioxin's toxicity (now under way), and once the new model of how it works is complete—EPA is seeking answers by May 1992—it may be possible to get a more accurate idea of the risk involved. As *Research News* concluded, "At this stage, no one is placing any bets, not even [leading dioxin researcher Michael] Gallo, who just ten months ago predicted that it would turn out to be far less risky than EPA now estimates. 'I have no idea how it will come out,' he says now." All this makes Tambrands' assurances less than comforting.

Cotton, the other principal ingredient in most brands of tampons, is also far from being environmentally perfect. One hundred and seventy insecticides are registered for use on cotton in the United States. A variety of these, along with heavy doses of herbicides, are applied to most of the American cotton crop at virtually every stage. Cotton is an extremely difficult crop to grow organically, although some headway is being made in California, Texas and Arizona (See Chapter 8). The bleaching sequence for cotton also has environmental drawbacks, including the use of formaldehyde.

So, if you're hooked on commercial tampons, you're stuck with a double whammy: tricky waste disposal problems and two principal ingredients—rayon and cotton—that haven't earned any ovations from environmentalists.

And from a health standpoint, tampons have other short-comings. The next chapter discusses toxic shock syndrome in detail, but there are other, less publicized problems with tampons. In Canada, the federal Bureau of Radiation and Medical Devices (you'll be relieved to know that tampons fall under the medical devices section) maintains a nationwide, twenty-four-hour toll-free hotline to keep track of all physician and consumer complaints (1-800-267-9675). Although this bureau wouldn't provide us with specifics, its records reveal a variety of tampon-related problems—foreign matter such as fragments of metal in tampons, loss of the withdrawal string (making the tampon difficult to remove), abdominal cramping, urinary tract infections, tampons breaking and shredding in the vagina, concerns about long-term effects and, of course, toxic shock syndrome.

There are other problems. American obstetrician-gynecologist Dr. Cynthia Cooke suspects that tampons are linked with chronic and recurrent vaginitis. Vaginal infections that had plagued an Ottawa friend of ours for months disappeared when she stopped using tampons.

Plastic applicators have sharp cusps that can lacerate the vaginal wall during insertion of the tampon, and all brands have been found to cause temporary dryness, cell peeling and even tiny ulcers. In an industry-sponsored study, Dr. Eduard Friedrich of the University of Florida College of Medicine found that most of the harmful effects did not last, but his research team concluded that repeated use of tampons, especially superabsorbents, could lead to micro-ulcers. Examination of some ulcer lesions have revealed tampon fibers imbedded in the vaginal wall.

Fragrance-laced tampons may cause skin irritation or allergic reactions and, in some cases, disrupt a woman's microbial balance, making her more susceptible to bacterial and yeast infections. Doctors and public health nurses advise against deodorant sanitary products. Jean Kern, a public health nurse who teaches health and sex education to primary grade and junior high school students in Sarnia, Ontario, was emphatic on this point. "I don't want them to use deodorant tampons. I try to explain that they are not necessary for proper hygiene and they're not good for their health." As she sees it, women are just adding needless chemicals to their bodies when they insert a baby powder-scented "plug."

Cloaking menstrual odor is the objective of deodorant or perfumed tampons. But this is totally unnecessary. Deodorized or not, tampons preclude odor by preventing menstrual blood from coming into contact with air. A strong or unusual odor is a sign of infection and should be treated, not masked. Playtex was the first company to introduce deodorant tampons to the American market, in 1971. It still stands as a textbook case of creating a need, then filling it. Playtex ads emphasize a woman's need to be discreet and worry-free. Tambrands' boxes of baby powder-scented tampons proclaim, "Extra gentle...help lessen the concern about menstrual odor so you can feel fresh and secure."

Women might feel more secure if we knew all of the ingredients manufacturers use in various tampons (well, better informed, anyway). Either way, we strongly believe we have a right to know what goes into our bodies. But tampon companies apparently have little interest in giving women extra comfort and security by listing their ingredients. In neither Canada nor the United States are sanitary product companies legally required to provide such a list, and—why aren't we surprised?—they don't.

We asked anyway, though. In fact, we sent letters to all the Canadian tampon and sanitary napkin companies requesting answers to a wide range of questions, including one about ingredients. Only one company, Tambrands, responded. It answered all of the questions we posed, even though some answers weren't very informative. The others—Johnson & Johnson Inc. (o.b. tampons, Sure & Natural and Stayfree pads), Playtex Ltd. (pink plastic applicator tampons) and Smith & Nephew Inc. (private-label tampons)—have remained silent to this day.

Dr. Cynthia Cooke, in her introduction to Nancy Friedman's 1981 book, *Everything You Must Know About Tampons*, states that tampon manufacturers and the American government have been "seriously remiss in accepting the veil of proprietary information and refusing to allow women to know exactly what they're putting in their bodies." She argues that women should be able to make informed decisions about these products: "Complete product labeling is an absolute prerequisite for making these decisions."

Ten years later, we're no better off. It's funny that labeling of ingredients in cosmetic products such as shampoo, nail polish and soap has been a legal requirement in the United States since 1976, but no similar law governs women's sanitary products. Lillian Yin, who is in charge of the Food and Drug Administration's Ob-Gyn-Dental devices branch in the U.S., delivers a long list of reasons why the FDA isn't going to compel disclosure. She said that it would involve rule-making, which would take too much time and invite criticism from industry (!).

Canada is in the same boat. The Bureau of Radiation and Medical Devices is not about to mandate the labeling of ingredients in tampons or sanitary pads, according to Bill Welsh, who heads up the pre-market review division. No explanation really. We get the sense that the government just can't be bothered.

Some companies do mention a few ingredients voluntarily on the box. In the United States, Tambrands lists cotton fiber, rayon fiber and overwrap, cotton cord and "fragrance" (a generic term) for its superabsorbent product. Playtex superabsorbency "portables" have rayon, polysorbate-20, a cotton string and may contain cotton fiber. Ms. Yin from the FDA confirmed that these aren't the only ingredients in the products but didn't seem concerned that women might think they were getting the full story. "Common sense tells women that they're not listing all of the ingredients," she said. Wrong. Common sense would lead most people to believe any list is a complete list—why would it be partial?

Tambrands Canada is planning to expand its list of ingredients soon. Right now, some product packaging states that its tampons are made from hygienic cotton and rayon fibers. The company is also considering promoting its all-cotton regular unscented product—as a totally natural product?—but once again, the other ingredients will be a mystery.

While government and private industry show little interest in disclosing a tampon's ingredients, others have managed to find them out. Lydia Cain writes in a 1989 issue of the journal, *Non-wovens world*, that tampons are made mostly of carded, resin-bonded rayon (resin-bonded means that the rayon fibers are held together with resin-based adhesives). A 1981 FDA study identified some of the materials that have been found to leach out of tampons—elements such as magnesium, boron, aluminum and titanium, along with numerous organics including acids, alcohols, amines and hydrocarbons. Waxes and surfactant-like compounds were present in all brands. (Surfactants are chemical substances that enhance the "wetting" properties or absorbency of the fiber.) By weight, residues accounted for almost 4 percent of a Playtex Regular Deodorant tampon, mostly due to fragrance additives.

A patent filed in the United States by German inventors Werner Schneider and Scarlet Sustmann gives us another hint of possible ingredients. "The impregnation of sanitary hygiene products with disinfectants, medicaments or fragrances to prevent as much as possible the occurrence of unpleasant odor is well known. For this purpose, phenols, mercuric chloride and sulfurous acid as well as various bactericides and fungicides...have been added to the absorbent layers of sanitary hygiene products."

Surfactants are a common component in tampons. Lillian Yin of the FDA says most tampons are treated with the surfactant polysorbate or Tween-20 to improve absorbency. Playtex Family Products in the U.S. lists this ingredient on its package, while Tambrands Canada uses a surfactant that it calls a "wetting agent." Tambrands said it uses these "federally approved" wetting agents in "very low concentrations."

When the tampon is inserted, surfactants come into direct contact with the vaginal wall. Yet toxicity data on these compounds are almost nonexistent, according to Dr. Ed Natke, former chief of the Product-Related Disease Division with Health and Welfare Canada (former because this division no longer exists, a victim of the trend toward reduced government vigilance over product safety). Dr. Natke says these surfactants, which are also widely used in cosmetic products, have been considered "inert" by the vast majority of people but, in his opinion, there's no such thing as inert when you're talking about human interaction with a substance. "It's not like putting it in a test tube," he says.

So much for "*toute naturellement.*"

On the face of it, tampons seem like the natural choice for women who are trying to step lightly on the earth. They're biodegradable, compostable (although only in the few places where municipal composting systems exist) and weigh only a few grams. Compared to plastic-lined and overpackaged sanitary pads, tampons seem to make better environmental sense, except maybe for those infernal plastic applicators and individual wrappers.

Yet they fail in so many other ways. If only tampons were free of dioxins, didn't carry the risk of toxic shock syndrome, were made with unbleached, organic cotton, contained nothing (such as rayon) produced with chlorine gas, had no other additives and were all fragrance-free. But they're not.

Convenience can no longer be the only criterion for tampons. North American women spend more than half a billion dollars annually on these products, and we have a right to know that they're both personally and environmentally safe. With relentless consumer pressure, mountains will move... and tampons will change.

6

Tampons, part two: Toxic shock syndrome— too high a price

In the spring of 1980, doctors and public health officials in Canada and the United States were baffled. They had a new, life-threatening disease on their hands. Patients, mainly young women, were arriving at hospital emergency departments displaying remarkably similar symptoms—high fever, vomiting, low blood pressure and a strange, sunburn-like rash. Many were in shock and experiencing kidney and liver failure; some later died.

As the number of cases climbed, a common pattern emerged. Almost all of the patients were menstruating women using tampons. This seemingly innocuous product was implicated as a major factor in the disease called toxic shock syndrome, or TSS.

By January, 1981, 942 cases of TSS, including forty deaths, had been confirmed in the United States. By the end of that year, sixty-one cases had emerged in Canada, with three deaths. Although these statistics are ten years old, and most women consider this disease a thing of the past, toxic shock syndrome is definitely *not* history.

In June, 1989, seventeen-year-old Alice Corman-Dunn of Sarnia, Ontario, was rushed to hospital severely ill with a high fever, vomiting and diarrhea. She died the following day after suffering a cardiac arrest and lapsing into a coma. Doctors testifying at the coroner's inquest held in December, 1990, said that the cause of Corman-Dunn's death was a bacterial infection that led to an acute inflammation of her internal organs. They further stated that Corman-Dunn died of menstrually related toxic shock syndrome.

What makes TSS so frightening is how quickly the disease can progress. Gladys Dunn, Alice's mother, still can't get over how rapidly her daughter became gravely ill. "She came home from a college interview complaining of a fever and sick stomach, so we put her to bed. When I went to look in on her the next morning, it was too late. She was almost gone."

TSS also struck Debra Johnson of Indianola, Iowa, with devastating speed on May 9, 1991. Debbie felt as if she were getting the flu, so husband Jerry drove her to the doctor, who administered an injection of antibiotics and sent her home. Then Jerry went off to work his shift as a service technician for Iowa Power. When he returned home about midnight, Jerry didn't recognize his wife who, in less than twelve hours, had become comatose and so severely bloated her eyes were swollen shut. She was burning up with a high fever.

Debbie was rushed by helicopter to Des Moines' Mercy Hospital Medical Center, where critical care doctors fought to save her life. They were successful, but the price has been extreme. The story of her ordeal was told in detail by Deborah Cushman, health reporter for the Des Moines *Register*, who spent weeks at the bedside of this TSS victim following

Johnson's admission to hospital. In Cushman's Friday, July 5, 1991, *Register* article, she reported:

Debbie has endured a weeks-long nightmare involving a battery of specialists, ranging from neurologists to kidney experts, and three surgeries, including amputation of her toes and many fingers. She *may* walk again by using foam inserts in her shoes, says another of her specialists.

"She resembled a victim who had suffered burns on 50 percent of her body," notes Dr. Eugene Cherny, Johnson's plastic surgeon. "She lost so much skin on her legs we had to perform grafts, and she lost a lot of skin on her chest."

Her kidneys failed, then gradually began to function again.

Debbie has been speechless for more than a month due to surgery and tubes into her body. Her hair has fallen out and she is virtually deaf.

We communicated by special telephone with Debbie Johnson in mid-November, 1991, several months after her discharge from hospital. She *is* able to walk with the help of a cane, but remains profoundly deaf. At the time of our "conversation," Debbie was about to undergo medical tests to see if she was a good candidate for an artificial cochlear implant, a device that helps deaf people pick up a semblance of human speech. Her advice to women using menstrual products is simple: "Stay away from every brand of tampons on the market until they can prove them safe for women." The Johnsons were also considering legal action against Playtex, the manufacturer of the tampon Debbie was using at the time of her grim experience with TSS.

How can an innocent-looking device like a tampon be implicated in health catastrophes such as these? It's as ludicrous as getting "mortal wounds from a pillow fight," in the words of Tom Riley. Riley is an Iowa lawyer who to date has taken on tampon manufacturers in well over one hundred TSS cases, including the landmark Patricia Kehm lawsuit which Riley wrote about in his book, *The Price of a Life*. This is a revealing and disturbing account of how Procter & Gamble used its massive resources to defend the now-infamous Rely tampon in a suit brought by Patricia Kehm's husband, Mike, after his wife died of TSS in September, 1980, just days before P & G reluctantly pulled Rely off the market.

While scientists don't know exactly how and why TSS occurs, they do know the following: the culprit is a toxin-producing form of the bacteria, *Staphylococcus aureus*, which is a common and usually benign resident of the nose, skin and vagina. In rare cases, and for reasons still not understood, this bacteria mysteriously multiplies and produces a potent toxin that has been found in at least 90 percent of the menstruating women who developed TSS. Nearly all were using tampons.

The role played by tampons in promoting TSS isn't fully understood either. But scientists believe tampons act as a perfect host for the *Staph aureus* bacteria, because they absorb menstrual blood and provide a "good" surface for the bacteria to colonize. Inserting a tampon also adds oxygen to the normally anaerobic (oxygen-free) environment in the vagina. Scientists have shown that oxygen stimulates production of the TSS toxin.

It's estimated that 5 to 15 percent of women have the *Staph aureus* bacteria in their vaginas at any one time, but it can be present one month and gone the next. It's also known that some women—especially young women—are more susceptible to toxic shock syndrome than others. While most people develop a natural immunity to the toxin, TSS patients apparently don't have antibodies that offer adequate protection. Men and children can get TSS too, from influenza, insect bites, skin lacerations and boils.

Many people wonder why menstrually related toxic shock syndrome only surfaced in 1980, although women had been using tampons for decades. It's a good question. To understand, a brief history of the modern-day tampon may help.

Women began using mass-produced tampons in the early 1930s. This new product, invented by a Colorado doctor, was made from compressed surgical cotton. In 1936, Tampax Incorporated bought the patent and began marketing the product for its liberating qualities—no more bulky pads and belts. Advertising told women that it was now possible to wear tight pants, go swimming any time of the month, and to lead a "normal life" without fear of "embarrassing leakage and odor."

By the 1970s, tampons were closing in on sanitary napkins as women's preferred menstrual product. But the traditional tampon made of compressed fibers had one serious drawback. When fully saturated, it had a tendency to leak (well, flood in some cases). Procter & Gamble, the giant corporation that manufactures mega-brands such as Crest toothpaste, Tide detergent, Noxema skin cream and, of course, Pampers and Luvs disposable diapers, saw this problem as a marketing opportunity and set out to design a fully absorbent and leakproof tampon.

Instead of using conventional pressed cotton, Procter & Gamble scientists created a product that closely resembled a tea bag and stuffed it full of synthetic fibers, including polyester sponges and chips of carboxy-methyl-cellulose (CMC). It was a revolutionary change in tampon design and the advertisements proudly proclaimed that it "absorbs even the worry." P & G christened the new product "Rely" and in 1975 began testing the waters by marketing it in small, select regions of the U.S.

As Pamela Sherrid reported in *Fortune* magazine in 1981, Procter & Gamble's move quickly sparked an absorbency race among Rely's competitors. Other manufacturers soon started adding their own mix of superabsorbent fibers to their products. Building on its regional successes, P & G finally rolled Rely out across the U.S. and Canada in early 1980.

All tampon brands were implicated when reports of toxic shock syndrome began pouring into the Atlanta Centers for Disease Control (CDC) in the spring and summer of that year. But further research singled out P & G's Rely as an "increased risk." The synthetics in the product swelled when wet, creating what appeared to be a perfect culture for bacteria during menstruation. A second CDC study showed that women who had "relied" on Rely exclusively during their periods accounted for almost three-quarters of the menstrually related TSS cases.

In September, 1980, Procter & Gamble quietly ceased production of Rely. Nevertheless, according to Tom Riley's book, *The Price of a Life*, P & G was tempted to keep right on selling the product since Rely was starting to close in on Tampax, the market leader—a frightening case of profits versus ethics.

Unfortunately, early hopes that the removal of Rely would signal the end of TSS quickly evaporated. Confirmed toxic shock syndrome cases which struck menstruating women continued to mount—nearly six hundred were recorded in the United States during 1981.

By that year, research had found absorbency to be a key risk factor for tampon-related TSS. In a project called the Tri-State Study, researchers concluded that the "users of high absorbency tampons have a greater risk of contracting TSS than users of low absorbency tampons." So Rely wasn't the only culprit—any high absorbency tampon increased a woman's risk of contracting TSS. Playtex's Super Plus product was shunted into the "high risk" category. Women using this particular tampon had a fifteen times greater chance of developing TSS than women using any other brand.

Despite the apparent medical dangers, "high risk" tampons loaded with synthetic materials such as polyacrylate and "enhanced" rayon continued to be marketed by Procter & Gamble's competitors for many years. Playtex aggressively advertised its Super Plus tampon as the most absorbent available—which it was, logging in with an absorbency rating of seventeen, slightly less than Rely's nineteen.

Following the TSS outbreak, Tambrands in the U.S. resurrected its "natural" 100 percent cotton Original Regular style: "No super-absorbent synthetic materials…no petro-chemical sponges," declared the ads. However, Tambrands quietly retained superabsorbents in its other products.

In February, 1985, a federal jury sitting in Wichita, Kansas, ordered International Playtex to pay more than eleven million dollars in damages to the family of TSS victim Betty

Ogilvie. This huge damage award was due in part to the jury's finding that Playtex had shown reckless disregard for the lives of women by continuing to promote and sell its high-absorbency polyacrylate-filled product. The judge in this case translated the jury's verdict and damage award into a clear message to the company: "Take your damnable product off the market—it's killing people."

Playtex and Tambrands appear to have heeded this tough message. They both switched over to a cotton-rayon blend for their products soon after. In doing so, they decreased over-all absorbency by about 25 percent. Tampon absorbency is now within the six- to fifteen-gram range compared to ten to twenty grams in the early 1980s, a substantial improvement from the days of the superabsorbent synthetics.

Tampon-related TSS has been with us for more than a decade now and, over the years, some important patterns have emerged that shed light on its risk factors:

- Women under thirty are most at risk, especially teenage girls between the ages of fifteen and nineteen. They haven't yet built up immunities to the toxin.
- Continuous, uninterrupted use of tampons over the course of even a single day increases a woman's chances of con-tracting the disease by a factor of thirty-three. This suggests that women should, at the very least, alternate between tampons and other options (i.e., sanitary pads) to reduce their risk.
- As we mentioned earlier, risk rises with absorbency. The more absorbent the tampon, the greater the chances of contracting the disease. Researchers now say that for every

additional gram of liquid a tampon can absorb, the risk of TSS rises by 37 percent. If you buy tampons, using the lowest possible absorbency is crucial to preventing TSS. It's safer to use a less-absorbent tampon and change it more often than to use the highly absorbent types like "super" and "super-plus."

Today, the Centers for Disease Control in Atlanta estimate that one to two menstruating women in every one hundred thousand will contract TSS. However, the Food and Drug Administration, which regulates tampons in the United States, cautions that the actual incidence of TSS can only be estimated and says that a higher risk of between one and seventeen per one hundred thousand menstruating women represents a reasonable estimate. Although TSS does strike men, children and women who aren't menstruating, women using tampons still account for about 70 percent of the total number of TSS cases.

It's always wise to be dubious about statistics, and we think TSS statistics warrant extra skepticism. Doctors in the United States are required to report all TSS cases to the Centers for Disease Control, but a minority actually do. Dr. Arthur Reingold, professor of epidemiology at the University of California at Berkeley, says statistics compiled by disease centers are "generally unreliable." Even in 1980 and 1981, when media coverage of TSS was at an all-time high, the CDC concluded it was hearing about only 15 percent of all cases. What's more, the few statistics we do have reflect only the severest cases of TSS. The CDC has set up the following "case definition" of the syndrome, and only those cases that meet the definition are recorded: a fever of 38.9°C (102° F) and a rash, followed by peeling of the skin two weeks after onset, low blood pressure and involvement of three major organ systems. So, milder cases, those involving only two major organ systems, for instance, wouldn't be recorded by the CDC.

Dr. Philip Tierno, Jr., a longtime TSS researcher with the New York University Medical Center believes that the CDC case definition is no longer workable because it doesn't reflect the true incidence of TSS among women who are tampon users. Dr. Tierno maintains that most of the cases of TSS he sees today don't reach the full-blown stage of the syndrome. For every case that does fit the CDC criteria, he sees five to seven more that do not. All of these "milder" cases—some of which are still very serious—go unrecorded by the CDC.

If tampon absorbency has gone down significantly and manufacturers have stopped using the more exotic synthetic fibers, why is tampon-related TSS still with us? Dr. Tierno believes he has at least a partial answer. "Pre-1975 tampons were less absorbent and made primarily of cotton." With the arrival of Rely, superabsorbent materials invaded the market. While the tampon makers have removed most of these synthetics from their products, Dr. Tierno maintains they have not gone far enough. "They're still using rayon." Dr. Tierno is convinced that manufacturers must remove rayon from tampons. Research he conducted with fellow microbiologist Bruce Hanna indicates that viscose rayon enhances the production of the TSS toxin much more than cotton. Earlier work by Dr. Merlin Bergdoll at the University of Wisconsin in 1983 supports this finding.

Other research negates these conclusions. In a laboratory study sponsored by Playtex Family Products, researchers with Rockefeller University in New York compared the production of the TSS toxin in cotton and rayon fibers and could find no difference between the two. Unfortunately, it's hard to comment on the significance or value of this research— the scope of the study was extremely small.

Canadian health officials reacted to the rising incidence of toxic shock syndrome by moving on two fronts. First, in December 1980, Health and Welfare Canada instructed tampon companies to print a warning on the outside of tampon boxes advising women of the TSS-tampon link. Six months later, the agency added tampons to its list of "high risk" medical devices such as heart pacemakers and intrauterine devices (IUDs). By putting tampons into this higher risk category, they became subject to a new, premarket review requirement. Tampon companies that wanted to change their product or introduce an entirely new brand had to submit safety data, including details about quality control, performance and results from lab and animal studies. Health and Welfare Canada's stamp of approval was necessary before any new or "improved" tampon hit the store shelf.

Unfortunately, tampons already on the market didn't have to be scrutinized. Although Health and Welfare did ask manufacturers to submit data on their existing brands in 1981, formal approval of these products wasn't required.

Awareness about toxic shock syndrome is hard to gauge. The doctors, public health nurses and health advocates we spoke to sense women aren't well-informed about the disease. U.S. public health researchers Diane Witzig and

Sharon Ostwald conducted the only study we could find on TSS awareness among adolescent women. Their survey, carried out in 1983, revealed that knowledge of TSS was limited, fragmented and inaccurate. Our own informal survey, though hardly scientific, was revealing: one woman told us "that women never die of toxic shock syndrome anymore." Others had only a vague notion of TSS, and seemed unsure of its causes and symptoms. The coroner's jury in the inquest into Alice Corman-Dunn's death from TSS recommended better education in schools, health clinics and the media, and changes to tampon packaging and advertising to raise women's awareness about TSS.

Classroom instruction about TSS prevented the death of one twelve-year-old girl in 1985. As reported in the *Washington Post*, she was able to recognize her symptoms—her mother thought she had the flu—removed her tampon and immediately contacted her doctor, ultimately saving her own life.

Sanitary protection companies, including Johnson & Johnson, Procter & Gamble and Tambrands, all distribute "educational" materials in schools. Tambrands is by far the most active, issuing brochures, videos, posters and sending their own consultants into classrooms. Most of the information focuses on puberty and the onset of menstruation, but companies lose no opportunity to promote brand name products.

Susan Cochrane, then Vice-President of Marketing at Tambrands Canada (her position was eliminated in a company reorganization in mid-1991) stated frankly that its educational program is geared to giving Tampax the competitive advantage with teenage girls, a goal echoed in the company's 1990 annual report. "The importance of teens to the continued growth of our Tampax franchise is clear. This is the age when women make their long-term choice of feminine protection product, forming the basis for the strong brand loyalty in the tampon category."

Tambrands goes on to explain that its education strategy is threefold: 1) primarily to educate young teens about puberty and menstruation; 2) to explain tampon use to female teens and promote trial usage of Tampax tampons; and 3) to direct first-time users to the best Tampax product for their needs. The company's classroom consultants make sure toxic shock is mentioned. A recently published brochure produced by Tambrands called *The Inside Story* contains two pages about TSS. This marks a big improvement over the earlier version, which had nothing at all about the syndrome although it was used in the years following the TSS "crisis" of 1980-81.

The authors of *The Curse: A Cultural History of Menstruation* suggest that manufacturers' failure to include information and warnings points to the less-than-educational nature of these company-sponsored publications. Selling the product, we are shockingly reminded, is the real bottom line!

We were dismayed to see that the Ontario government's publication on adolescence and growing up completely omits any mention of TSS in the section that deals with sanitary napkins and tampons. The author, a senior medical consultant, defended this deliberate omission by pointing out that a girl has a greater risk of being run over by a car than getting toxic shock syndrome from tampons. Teaching them about TSS would only lead to unnecessary anxiety, she added. "Why put thousands of young girls in fear of using tampons?" This is a neanderthal attitude, needless to say, especially since the fifteen- to nineteen-year-old age group is the highest risk category for menstrually related TSS. The number of young women who contract AIDS is far lower than those who get TSS, yet education about AIDS is more widespread and more thorough.

Like AIDS, toxic shock syndrome is largely preventable, but prevention depends on awareness of the disease and its symptoms. A good place to start would be more distinct TSS warnings on tampon packaging. (If they can do it for cigarettes, why not tampons?) The small print on today's packages has frustrated and angered women who have fallen sick with the syndrome, including Laura Harker of Agincourt, Ontario, who nearly died after contracting a serious case of the disease in 1987. After she recovered, she complained that the package warning was simply not prominent enough. Many others have made the same complaint. Health and Welfare Canada requires a special message about TSS inside tampon packages—a good idea—but we think it should be accompanied by bolder warnings outside.

Absorbency has long been recognized as a key risk factor in TSS—the higher the absorbency, the greater the risk. So if a woman wanted to be cautious, she would naturally choose a Slender or Regular tampon, assuming they represent the lowest absorbency available. But, until recently, the terms Regular, Super and Super Plus were meaningless. Why? They weren't standard from brand to brand. Gladys Dunn, Alice Corman-Dunn's mother, points out that Super tampons were prohibited in their household. "We only used Playtex Regular," she said, but she couldn't know that a Playtex *Regular* had the same absorbency as a Tampax *Super*, based on

American statistics from 1987. Both could absorb the same amount of liquid—nine grams.

In 1988, the Washington-based Public Citizen Health Research Group launched a lawsuit against the U.S. Food and Drug Administration, charging that the FDA had failed to adequately regulate tampon labeling and absorbency. During the course of the suit, the FDA admitted that the labels were grossly inadequate. The court ordered the agency to produce a mandatory absorbency standard and define terms such as Regular and Super. "Without this regulation," the court stated, "women will continue to needlessly subject themselves to the risk of serious injury and even death from toxic shock syndrome, and they will remain deprived of information they need to make knowledgeable decisions about selecting tampons."

Almost ten years after the link between high absorbency tampons and TSS was first established, the FDA finally brought out its classification regulation. It assigned specific ranges of absorbency to the terms Junior, Regular and Super. For example, Super tampons must absorb between nine and twelve grams of liquid. The outer package must include an explanation of absorbency ranges, and more important, tell women that they can reduce their risk of TSS by choosing low absorbency tampons. We advise women to err on the side of caution and choose a less absorbent tampon.

Canada followed in the American government's footsteps, but only went part way. Officials from Health and Welfare Canada worked out a voluntary agreement with tampon companies about absorbency standards and labeling, identical to the FDA regulations. By December, 1990, all new production of Canadian tampons conformed to the new absorbency standards. But the Canadian agreement fell short, particularly with respect to the TSS warning on the outside packaging. Looking at most Canadian tampon boxes "before and after," you'd never know a change had taken place. Unlike their American counterparts, Canadian companies aren't required to explain the new absorbency ranges or to tell women they can reduce their risk of TSS by choosing a lower absorbency product. This warning *must* go on all U.S. products. The Canadian version of Johnson & Johnson's o.b. comes closest to what the FDA requires in the U.S.—it includes a graph illustrating the new standardized ranges and absorbencies.

Tambrands Canada ran a series of advertisements to inform consumers of the industry's move to standardize tampons, telling women it's important to choose the lowest absorbency to meet their needs. Just one thing was missing—there wasn't a single mention of toxic shock syndrome!

As a trade-off for tampon companies' voluntary agreement to standardize labeling, Health and Welfare Canada downgraded their products from the "high risk" category of medical devices to the "general" division. This offer isn't surprising considering the current philosophy of Health and Welfare bureaucrats in Ottawa. Albert Liston, head of Health and Welfare's Health Protection Branch, who put forward the proposal, often talks of the government's retreat from the big stick mentality. "Cooperation with industry" and "voluntary compliance" are the buzzwords of the day.

Thomas Henter, an evaluator with the Bureau of Radiation and Medical Devices, said the government is also thinking about removing "many other" high-risk devices, such as heart pacemakers, from the premarket review classification. Why tampons? Henter answered that voluntary standards are in place and that tampons are manufactured by "a stable industry making clean and usable products." Henter added that some people are not satisfied that there is a "causal relationship between tampons and toxic shock syndrome. It's still inconclusive," he said. Where has he been? The statistics clearly show otherwise.

If Canadian tampons are removed from the high risk category, they'll be in the same group as tongue depressors, dental floss and bandages. Tampon manufacturers who change fibers or fragrances or create a whole new product design will be under no obligation to obtain government approval—they'll simply notify the bureau that they're available for sale in Canada.

In Japan, tampons and sanitary napkins must conform to standards set by the Ministry of Health and Welfare. They must be free of dyes, fluorescence, acids and alkalis. They must absorb a certain minimum amount of fluid within a specified length of time, and leave only a 1 percent residue after being boiled and filtered. Furthermore, tampons and their withdrawal strings must be strong enough to withstand being pulled at a certain tension. And the list goes on. Canada has strict standards for condoms which, to the best of our knowledge, have never killed anyone. For heaven's sake, why not tampons?

If the Canadian government goes ahead with deregulation, what would prevent another Rely from happening? Tampon manufacturers have less than enviable records when it comes to protecting women consumers. Procter & Gamble was forced out of the market in the wake of the Rely disgrace, but it hasn't necessarily left for good. Scientists at the P & G labs in Cincinnati continue to study toxic shock syndrome. A summary of their findings was published in a 1989 edition of the journal *Reviews of Infectious Diseases*. We also discovered that this multibillion-dollar multinational bought a tampon design patent in 1984, four years after the disappearance of Rely.

Will TSS history repeat itself?

EARLY SYMPTOMS OF
TOXIC SHOCK SYNDROME

Courtesy of the Women's Environmental Network,
Great Britain

Early TSS symptoms resemble flu and include:

- sudden high fever, around 102° F or 38.9° C, or higher
- nausea
- vomiting
- diarrhea
- sore throat
- aching muscles
- dizziness, fainting or near fainting when standing up
- sunburn-like peeling rash, especially on hands and feet

If you have any of these symptoms and are using a tampon, remove it and contact your doctor for immediate treatment. Tell your doctor you have been using tampons and think that you may have TSS.

The acute phase of TSS progresses with a rapid loss of blood pressure (hypotension), toxins oozing from orifices, shedding skin (desquamation), respiratory failure and kidney failure. Necrosis (a decay of cells caused by poor blood supply) can cause the loss of fingers and toes. Aftereffects can include hair and fingernail loss, double vision, headaches, deafness, a loss of concentration and arthritis. These effects can last for months, years or, in some cases, permanently.

7
Whitewash: Everything but the whole truth

We picked the title of this book for obvious reasons—to drive home the idea that we're awash in a sea of bright white bleached paper products, and to stress the crucial connection with chlorine. Chlorine bleaching = bright white = pollution, and lots of it. Simple.

But as we worked away at this project, "whitewash" began taking on a whole new—and equally disturbing—meaning for us. What shakes out from our whole writing experience is, above all, a discomforting slew of misinformation. We encountered everything from subtle sins of omission and shifty public relations ploys through to bold and deliberate deceptions, all in the name of protecting profits and preserving business and all at the expense of a safer environment and women's health.

Sins of omission start with the sanitary product manufacturers. We wrote letters asking a series of straightforward questions about a variety of product-related issues—what kind of pulp each company uses, whether its raw materials are chlorine-bleached, what other "ingredients" are contained in their brands and so on. Then, we waited, and waited...but nothing except empty mailboxes greeted us. We eventually got the message: what these companies do is none of our business, and we don't have the right to know. The answers that finally did appear were basically brush-offs, loaded with phrases like "trade secrets" and "proprietary information." Kimberly-Clark in Toronto sent along a PR piece entitled "Kimberly-Clark Talks About Dioxin," but when we asked for more information, the company refused to give us specifics.

Some credit is due here to Tambrands and Procter & Gamble, the industry giants producing tampons and disposable diapers, respectively. Both companies tried to respond to our queries and concerns, and we're grateful even if we *don't* approve of their products. Not surprisingly, they bear the brunt of our heaviest criticisms, simply because they were the only companies which gave us enough information to criticize! As for the rest—Playtex, Johnson & Johnson, Kimberly-Clark, and Cascades, to name a few—the lack of response was disconcerting and disturbing.

The whitewash with women's menstrual products begins with language like "sanitary protection" and "feminine hygiene." We now know that "sanitary" pads, tampons and disposable diapers are not "clean," that bleaching them whiter than white with chlorine defiles both the environment and the products themselves with the most insidious kind of contaminants.

On the diaper front, makers of disposables have pulled out all the stops in a down and dirty struggle to hold on to or expand their market share. Take two of Procter & Gamble's magazine advertisements, for example. As we discussed in

Chapter 4, one boldly proclaims: "The new life cycle of a disposable diaper." The accompanying illustrations depict the P & G diaper degenerating quickly into compost, eventually even sprouting a seedling, while the captions describe the "action": "Currently our diapers are 80 percent compostable. The plastic is separated from the diaper. The diaper is broken down in the municipal compost heap. Finally, the compost is used as a soil conditioner."

The Recycling Council of Ontario, joined by seven other environmental groups, has asked the Canadian government to investigate this advertisement. Facilities producing compost from disposable diapers simply don't exist in Canada, the Council says, insisting that widespread, publicly accessible composting programs must be in place before P & G can claim its product is 80 percent compostable. Makes sense to us. Meanwhile, New York City's Consumer Affairs Commissioner has also taken action against Procter & Gamble for a similar ad, citing "deceptive trade practice." The verdict in this case was that P & G, while admitting no wrongdoing, agreed that it would not run the ad again and promised it would not make unqualified claims about the compostability of its diapers until the proper facilities were widely available in New York City. Procter & Gamble also picked up the $5,000 cost of the investigation (very small change indeed for a company reporting profits of more than $1.6 billion in 1990).

Here's another questionable Pampers advertisement. "To the environment, it's six of one, half a dozen of the other. But to a baby, there's a clear winner." Suggesting that there's a toss-up environmentally between paper and cloth diapers,

P & G implies that parents should make a choice based on its claim that disposables are the winner in another arena: the battle against diaper rash.

In a letter to the Toronto Board of Health, Craig Gammie of Kimberly-Clark Canada wrote that "disposable diapers offer health benefits unmatched by cloth diapers." His counterpart at Procter & Gamble, Dennis Darby, made a similar claim: "Disposable diapers offer significant health benefits." Both point to clinical studies that demonstrate less rash with disposables than cloth. The Ontario Medical Association and others including Toronto's Medical Officer of Health challenge these claims. The OMA's Committee on Child Welfare did its own review of the medical literature and concluded, "Although there may be slightly less rash with the disposable diapers, for children with normal skin, cloth diapers are more than adequate." Hardly "unmatched" or "significant."

In Britain, the Women's Environmental Network (WEN) recently lodged a complaint with the Advertising Standards Authority, questioning a total of twenty-three claims Procter & Gamble made in leaflets and brochures for its Pampers product. WEN is challenging—and we are too—the claim that cloth diapers have only a slight environmental advantage over disposables, based on its industry-sponsored "life-cycle" studies.

The London *Guardian* reports how Procter & Gamble was forewarned about the WEN complaint and tried to do some early "damage control." Internal P & G memoranda obtained by the *Guardian* reveal that the company made plans to retaliate with "our emergency environmental equivalence mailing," whatever that means. The article goes on to say that

P & G also tried to obtain a copy of WEN's submission before publication and drew up a list of "press people to target."

On this side of the ocean, Carol Pickup, a Victoria-area municipal councillor, told us how Procter & Gamble reacted when she proposed a ban on landfilling of disposable diapers in her locality. "They blanketed the area with samples of baby diapers. It was indiscriminate. Even old-age homes received them in the mail. They were sent all over the greater Victoria area and even to parts of Vancouver." In our view, this is widespread whitewash of the worst kind. Only a mega-corporation like Procter & Gamble can afford this sort of campaign.

Language about pulping is, in our opinion, deliberately misleading. Take the expression "oxygen-bleached," for example. Surely this means the pulp is bleached with oxygen, eliminating the need for chlorine-based agents, correct? Wrong. What it means is that some of the woody lignin is removed using oxygen before the pulp is bleached with chlorine compounds.

Then there's "oxygen-based pulp bleaching." The same as "oxygen bleaching," right? No chlorine? Wrong again. It's a term used by Tambrands Canada to describe the bleaching process used by its rayon suppliers. When we asked for clarification, Tambrands Canada responded with what must surely win the prize for doublespeak:

We neither manufacture nor bleach the rayon used in our tampons. However, the pure cellulose (dissolving pulp) used by our vendor in the manufacture of rayon is obtained from wood pulp by a process that involves the use of chlorine gas and chlorine dioxide.

This process has undergone continuous modification since the mid-1980's resulting in significant reductions in the use of both chlorine gas and chlorine dioxide. Furthermore, with our encouragement, research is being actively pursued on processes which eliminate the use of chlorine gas. Substantial progress has been made, but a commercially acceptable process is not yet available. The rayon fibers are bleached by our vendors using dilute aqueous sodium hypochlorite at a low temperature. This is conducted under alkaline conditions that neither use nor produce elemental chlorine in the bleaching process. Under these conditions, oxygen, not chlorine, is the bleaching agent. Here too, alternative bleaching agents, e.g. hydrogen peroxide, are being explored.

We believe that the above information supports our statement that cotton and rayon fibers used in the manufacture of Tampax tampons are not chlorine bleached, but are in fact treated with oxygen-based bleaches.

Perfectly clear now?

With chlorine under increasing pressure, you're bound, of course, to see more claims of "chlorine-free." When we first heard the expression, we assumed—wrongly again—that the product was pulped and bleached without the use of any chlorine compounds—no chlorine gas, chlorine dioxide or hypochlorite. But makers of bright white pulp and paper products mean only that a product is chlorine-gas free; the other two compounds are still used in the process, but are not mentioned.

To avoid confusion, the new expression making the rounds for truly chlorine-free processes is "chlorine-compound free." Equally good (but even more of a mouthful) is "lightened without the use of any chlorine-based chemicals." Better still, manufacturers should tell us what they *do* use—such as hydrogen peroxide—rather than what they don't.

As we delved more deeply into the hotly debated dioxin issue, we began to view the role of science with suspicion. While the pulp and chemical industries have obvious vested interests to protect—we thought, naively perhaps, that science was somehow "without prejudice." Certainly there are dedicated scientists who work well beyond the range and influence of corporately sponsored research grants, but far fewer than we thought.

Much of the so-called scientific research into accidental exposure to dioxin has been exposed as fraudulent. Let's take a closer look at some of this research.

Chemical explosions involving dioxin at the Monsanto Company's Nitro, West Virginia, factory in 1949 and at a BASF West Germany plant in 1953 are two events that led to a series of human health studies. These in turn yielded what seemed to be evidence that no direct relationship exists between dioxin exposure and any health effects, aside from the skin disease chloracne. But chinks in this research have recently split wide open. West German epidemiologist Friedemann Rohleder took a second look at the exposed BASF workers and found significantly higher levels of respiratory cancer and cancer of the digestive tract. He also found that the original BASF studies, paid for by the company, were of questionable standards. Unexposed workers had been deliberately added to the "exposed" group, while several workers who had been exposed—and had symptoms of chloracne—were deliberately excluded from the study.

The Monsanto research is also under fire. Among other stinging critiques and scientific re-evaluations, a November, 1990 Greenpeace report entitled *Science for Sale* outlined ten examples of "improper conduct" in the Nitro studies, concluding: "As a result of these manipulations, the data and conclusions of the three Monsanto studies are essentially meaningless." At the time of writing, the U.S. Environmental Protection Agency was investigating the questionable Monsanto research to establish whether criminal charges should be laid.

But probably the most controversial dioxin research has involved Vietnam War veterans exposed to the defoliant Agent Orange and its potent dioxin contaminant. The U.S. Air Force conducted several studies beginning in 1978 and over the course of several years, released findings that were "reassuring." They showed "no evidence of a link between the health of study participants and exposure to herbicides in Vietnam."

This Air Force research, as congressional investigations later revealed, was grossly distorted by deliberate misclassifications in both the "exposed" and "control" groups. Despite these distortions, differences were still found between the two groups in nine categories of health effects, including all types of cancer. But this finding, as well as another revealing birth defects in the children of soldiers exposed to Agent Orange, was not disclosed in the Air Force's key 1984 report.

Retired U.S. Navy Admiral Elmo R. Zumwalt, Jr. was appointed by the American Department of Veterans Affairs to review the whole Agent Orange research fiasco. This is a man whose initial skepticism about dioxin was radically transformed by events. Zumwalt had commanded U.S. naval forces during the Vietnam War and was responsible for orders to spray Agent Orange in various parts of that country. Among the troops he sent in was his own son, Elmo R. Zumwalt III. When reports about links between chronic health problems and dioxin began to surface in the mid-1970s, Zumwalt rejected any cause-and-effect relationship. In 1983, his son contracted two types of cancer and, after a long struggle with the illness, died in August, 1988. Over that time, Admiral Zumwalt and his son came to believe these cancers were related to Agent Orange.

After accepting the invitation to head up the Agent Orange review project in 1989, Zumwalt appointed an informal group of experts to help him critique the human and animal studies done on the defoliant, and to research civilian exposure to dioxin contaminants. Here is a short segment of his final report:

It can, in my judgment, be concluded, with a very high degree of confidence, that it is at least as likely as not that the following are caused in humans by exposure to TCDD [tetra-chloro-dibenzo-p-dioxin]: non-Hodgkin's lymphoma, chloracne and other skin disorders, lip cancer, bone cancer, soft tissue sarcoma, birth defects, skin cancer, porphyria cutanea tarda and other liver disorders, Hodgkin's disease, hematopoietic diseases, multiple myeloma, neurological defects and auto-immune diseases and disorders, leukemia, lung cancer, kidney cancer, malignant melanoma, pancreatic cancer, stomach cancer, colon cancer, nasal/pharyngeal/esophageal cancers, prostate cancer, testicular cancer, liver cancer, brain cancer, psychosocial effects and gastrointestinal diseases.

Despite these compelling re-examinations of older dioxin studies, the statement "no proven effects other than chloracne," is constantly paraded out by those who have a vested interest in chlorine-based processes. While this may be technically correct—scientific "proof" requires rigorous methodology and repeatable results—no mention is ever made by industry of Admiral Zumwalt's report or the tainted human health studies.

"Half truths and half measures" best sums up the pulp and paper industry's role in the dioxin story. From the beginning, the American pulp and paper sector's handling of the dioxin situation has been less than open. It did not take meaningful action until Greenpeace released its *No Margin of Safety* report in 1987, at least four years after the discovery of the most potent dioxin in pulp mill effluent.

Fear of lost revenue was certainly one motive for keeping the matter under wraps. A poll commissioned quietly by the American Paper Institute (API) in 1986 confirmed that three out of five consumers might buy fewer bleached paper products if they contained traces of dioxin. What followed was a whole tangled web of secret agreements, tactics to stall dioxin regulation and public relations maneuvers to "keep all allegations of health risks out of the public arena—or minimize them," according to a leaked API document.

Whitewashing isn't solely an American art form. The Canadian pulp and paper industry has also contributed its fair share of misinformation since the dioxin scandal broke in 1987, even if outright fraud and deception aren't part of the package. Take just one example, a 1990 report by the Council of Forest Industries (COFI) in British Columbia which describes the environmental track record of the B.C. pulp and paper sector and its prospects for sustainable development. The picture painted in this document is a rosy one. But so flawed are its contents that two senior officials from Environment Canada felt compelled to set the record straight in their own report. This critique begins by congratulating COFI for providing an "excellent" description of the B.C. pulp and paper industry and its vital importance to the provincial economy, then continues: "It is, nonetheless, a document of debatable technical merit. The selective use of observations from source material, the omission of certain facts about issues raised in the paper, and a general lack of detail about assumptions used to calculate the estimated cost of adopting environmental controls, together, raise concern about the credibility of the report....There are many statements in the COFI paper which in our opinion could convey inaccurate impressions." From government officials, this is exceedingly strong language.

Just as the American pulp and paper industry failed to contain the dioxin issue, chlorine producers also tripped over their own fancy PR strategy. Since this industry supplies pulp and paper mills with tons of its product every year, it had obvious reasons—declining sales—to worry when those chlorine-based "accidents"—the dioxins and furans—were discovered in pulp mill effluent. The Washington-based Chlorine Institute decided that science could help immeasurably by reaching a consensus on "safe" levels of dioxin exposure, and created the perfect venue for this science-based program. It came to fruition in October, 1990, when thirty-eight of the world's leading experts on dioxin gathered at the respected Banbury Center at New York's Cold Spring Harbor Laboratory to discuss latest developments in dioxin research.

The Chlorine Institute's public relations firm sent out a controversial press release at the conclusion of the meeting, proclaiming that the experts had agreed on a model of toxicity for dioxin that "allows for the presence of the substance in the environment, with no risk experienced below a certain level of exposure...." Few of these scientists knew that the conference was sponsored by the chlorine industry, and when it was over, even fewer realized they had reached a consensus on anything. Banbury participant Dr. Ellen Silbergeld, dioxin researcher and visiting professor of toxicology at the University of Maryland, was incensed. In a letter to conference organizers, she angrily protested: "I agreed to participate based on my previously held high regard for Banbury and Cold Spring Harbor. I did not expect to be manipulated by industry and government spokespeople (who are not dioxin researchers, incidentally)...I do not feel that the state of knowledge on this complex topic can be reduced to a simplistic press release."

Despite the whirl of controversy, the U.S. Paper Industry Office hustled quickly to distribute information about the Banbury Conference "consensus" to pulp mills and the media, using it as a springboard for some highly dubious information for public consumption. "[I]t may be hard for the public to believe, but the latest and best scientific evidence shows that dioxin is enormously less dangerous to human health than had previously been believed," states a Paper Industry Office letter to newspaper reporters.

And here's one more "whitewash" tactic from the chlorine industry: Ketchum Communications, a U.S.-based public relations firm, developed a "Crisis Management Plan" for the Clorox Company, makers of household bleach. This plan, never instituted, was leaked to Greenpeace in May, 1991, and called for a variety of dubious tactics to deflect criticism away from Clorox if a crisis blew up—denouncing Greenpeacers as "environmental terrorists," exploring the possibility of libel or slander suits against news columnists who advocate nontoxic bleaches and recruiting "scientific ambassadors" to give credibility to Clorox's environmental messages.

The Crisis Plan also described how the ideal media spokesperson should come across. "It's important to remember that while substance is crucial, style, appearance and tone count as well. A sensitive spokesperson will always express concern about potential damage or inconvenience to the public. He/she will present a position that doesn't appear to be self-serving—sometimes using a disarming candor, other times presenting an understandable firmness."

Where's the truth in all this!

8
Ragtime revisited: The case for reusables

What is it about suggesting a switch to washable cotton menstrual pads or reusable tampons? Judging by the reaction of some women, reusable sanitary products are about as popular as the bubonic plague.

"Ask me to do anything else for the environment and I'm willing, but not *that*," one woman responded to our suggestion about considering reusables.

Well, if it's any consolation, both of us were caught on the horns of this very dilemma just six months before publication of this book. "Guess if we write this thing, we better start thinking about using reusable *somethings*," said Adrienne. "Maybe if I'm lucky, menopause will arrive a little early," Liz hoped quietly. (It was not to be.)

Now we can say, with conviction, confidence and pride, that switching over to reusable menstrual products is really not a big deal. In fact, both of us wonder why we'd made such a fuss.

"For many women, the big concern is how they'll care for reusable pads after years of just throwing the disposables away," says Lynn Burrows, founder of the reusable sanitary product company, Women's Choice, with headquarters on a six-acre farm in Gabriola, British Columbia. "'What will I do with these messy things?' they ask. The answer is simple: Soak them in a bucket of cold water, which dissolves the blood and prevents permanent staining, then run them through with the regular laundry. These pads wash up very easily, and they dry well, too."

Women working away from home have other concerns. "They wonder if reusable pads are appropriate, but it's just a matter of being prepared if you're out of the house for several hours. Store the used ones in an airtight bag until you get home; *then* toss them in a bucket of cold water," Lynn Burrows advises.

But bigger than worries about the care and maintenance of reusable pads, which is pretty simple after all, is the whole idea of acknowledging that women actually menstruate. Switching to reusables means we can't instantly flush tampons away or bury bundled-up pads in the bottom of the bathroom wastebasket. The very thought of somebody discovering our cold-water buckets tucked under the sink is terrifying. What will they think? What will we say? After all, it's almost bred in our bones to be infinitely discreet about this monthly "secret."

Almost. In reality, the marketers of disposable sanitary products have done a masterful job of playing up the "need" for prudence while convincing us that our periods can practically disappear—an amazing feat of advertising when you consider the word "menstruate" is never, ever mentioned, except in the required TSS warnings on tampon packaging.

Where did we westerners go astray? In some other cultures, menarche—the onset of menstruation—is cause for celebration, openly acknowledged as the beginning of fertility in a young woman's life. Grown women head happily off to the menstrual hut or gather on moss "couches" for a monthly break. Meanwhile, we dutifully plug ourselves up and carry on as if nothing is happening.

It is these two factors—the anticipated inconvenience plus our culturally induced anguish about this normal bodily function—that make the thought of reusables so difficult for many women, at least at first.

While changing from disposable paper diapers back to cloth is considered a step forward for the environment, reusable sanitary napkins are often dreaded as a loathsome throwback to bygone days of "the rag," abandoned with few regrets when single-use sanitary pads became widely available.

But times have certainly changed. "The cloth pads of the 1990s are far different from what our grannies had," says Liann Hartley, co-founder of Many Moons, a reusable sanitary napkin company based in Victoria, B.C. "We've improved on them—they're beautiful and soft. They're also comfortable and simple to use."

And flamboyant too, if that's your preference. Many Moons offers its pads in three color themes—"wild," an anything-but-restrained leopard skin pattern, as well as the more conservative "soft" and "plain" versions. "Beautiful florals, playful prints and rich solids" are offered by New Cycle Products of Santa Rosa, California, while vegetable-dyed Peach and Dusty Rose are the colors available from Women's Choice. Some rags!

But are you still skeptical? So was Eileen Smith, who sat at Liann Hartley's dining room table sewing the first reusables for Many Moons. "I thought she was crazy and figured it was never going to happen, that this 'business' would be a total failure. But the orders started coming and they're very steady. It took me ten months to try the pads I was helping to sew, and another four to convert completely. Now I actually don't mind getting my period. In fact, with the fancy lace-belted version of the Many Moons I use, it's kind of sexy." Spoken like a true convert.

Most reusable companies carry a range of products—standard, heavy and light flow pads, beltless and belted versions, and panty liners, even ones with wings. The reusables mimic many of the best features of throwaway pads without loading up landfill sites. Velcro fasteners are popular (although Eileen Smith swears they can't compare to the belted variety), and some companies offer other products, including totes, books on menstruation and female-cycle charts.

Most of the reusables we found are made from 100 percent cotton flannelette, usually with a moisture-proof backing, although fabrics will vary. Women's Choice opted for 100 percent cotton fleece, identical to the soft material you find inside jogging suits. "This is much more expensive than flannelette, but it's really absorbent and durable, lasting a minimum of five years," explains Lynn Burrows. Alternatively, the We Care line of sanitary pads are sewn from a 94 percent cotton/6 percent polyester blend of terrycloth by Waddles in White of Hamilton, Ontario, which—as its name aptly suggests—chiefly makes reusable diapers. Jan Dummer, the company's founder, explains that the polyester helps keep the terry soft and absorbent.

Cotton, although reusable and biodegradable (when it eventually wears out), has a less than enviable environmental record as an agricultural crop. Most cotton fields are doused with a slew of herbicides, insecticides, desiccants and defoliants—over forty million pounds were dumped on the 1982 American crop, reported Hannah Holmes recently in the environmental magazine, *Garbage*. (This excellent article was called "The Truth About Tampons.")

But without all these chemicals, some claim, the cotton crop would be a disaster. In a July, 1991, *New Yorker* story about crop-dusting in the Mississippi Delta, writer Donovan Webster claims that without pesticides and herbicides, "Forty percent of our national cotton harvest would be ruined by boll worm and boll weevil.... The cotton gins would stop."

Cotton farmer/botany professor Jerry Williams explained some of the problems to Webster. "Cotton is a difficult crop even for the oldest hands at it. We have huge insect and weed problems with cotton, and the plant itself is very delicate. There are pre-emergence herbicides to control grass and broadleaf weeds. There are seed treatments to protect the seed before it has germinated. Then, the instant the cotton comes up, it's attacked by insects. And that's a long battle..." Finally, when the crop is ready to harvest, planes swoop over to spray a defoliant that makes the leaves drop off so the cotton can be harvested more easily.

Still, it is possible to grow a successful crop without applying pesticides or herbicides. Sally Fox is a cotton "breeder" in California. She specializes in developing seeds for natural cotton colors, so that the fiber doesn't have to be bleached and dyed later, which she describes as a "very polluting" process.

Fox has already succeeded in breeding a consistent supply of seeds for brown and green cotton, and is now trying for terra cotta. This is exacting work that takes several seasons of cross-pollinating to get just the right combination of good color and decent fiber.

Fox grows her cotton organically in the San Joaquin Valley, a task that she says is easier in states such as California, Texas and Arizona than it is in the South. "In Mississippi, pests like the boll weevil are so ensconced that it's difficult to grow cotton without spray. Here we're using biological controls with a good degree of success, constantly releasing sterile boll weevils to keep populations in check. We're working with a really great entomologist who does all sorts of clever things like planting other crops alongside the cotton to feed the insects."

Weeds are another story, however. "There's no magic potion for them," Fox says. "They're very persistent, and very expensive to take out manually." But she's convinced that a method for growing organic cotton without the painstaking hand-weeding will be developed. "It took a long time to figure out the way to do organic vegetables, and it will evolve for cotton too."

Fox recently produced a crop of her brown organic cotton for use in New Cycle's reusable menstrual pads, the first totally natural cotton product we're aware of—no pesticides, no herbicides, no bleaches, no dyes. But if women demand them, this will be the first of many all-natural cotton products.

There are also sew-it-yourself reusable pads. An excellent pattern is found in a book called *Hygieia: A Woman's Herbal* by Jeannine Parvati (Freestone, 1978). The winter, 1991, edition of *Mothering* magazine also carried easy-to-follow instructions on how to make a cloth maxi-pad in an article called "Converting to Cloth" by Sue Smith-Heavenrich.

For die-hard tampon fans who worry about what all these disposables are doing to the environment but can't bear switching to sanitary pads, reusable alternatives are available for you too. The most natural are sea sponges. However, as Hannah Holmes reported in her article, "The Truth About Tampons," the American Food and Drug Administration subjected the sea sponge to a rough bureaucratic ride over a decade ago, and still does not permit it to be described as a menstrual product: "With uncharacteristic vigor, the FDA squashed small businesses that in the late '70s sold sea sponges for menstrual use...the FDA's Ms. [Lillian] Yin says the agency's concern was that women might rinse their sponges in public sinks." Furthermore, we should point out, sea sponges can be contaminated with sand, fungi, bacteria and chemicals from oil spills, and have also been linked to at least two cases of toxic shock syndrome.

We ordered some sponges by mail from a company in New Hampshire, asking how to use them as tampons. This was the characteristic reply: "We do not recommend, in any way, the use of silk cosmetic sponges for tampons.... We do not have any instruction for them as they are cosmetic sponges. Thank you."

Meanwhile, women continue to buy sponges regularly for use as tampons, despite the strict prohibition on the designation "menstrual product." (Funny that the big sanitary protection corporations, who can use this phrase, avoid it like the plague, while the sponge sellers are forbidden to use it, yet everybody still knows what they're selling. Must be ESP.)

A company in Port Lavaca, Texas, dances neatly around the

FDA restriction. "Several years ago, our sponges were sold as a 'menstrual sponge,'" its promotional literature says. "The FDA required us to remove this term from our label. We also no longer provide any instruction on their use…. We do still carry the same quality sponge we always have, but we must inform the consumer that we: GIVE NO WARRANTY OF THIS PRODUCT FOR ANY PARTICULAR USE. How you choose to use our sponge is completely your decision as a consumer. We feel it is important for you to have a choice." If you do buy sea sponges for menstrual use, the book, *The New Our Bodies, Ourselves*, by the Boston Women's Health Collective, provides excellent guidelines for their use and maintenance.

From the book, *The Curse: A Cultural History of Menstruation*, comes this handy idea: "Following the advice of Alicia Bay Laurel in *Living on the Earth*, we made our own tampons out of a [household] sponge. One 12 cent O-Cel-O kitchen sponge (3 1/2 by 4 3/4 inches) divided widthwise into four equal strips makes four perfect tampons…. It is by far the best protection not on the market…."

Another alternative to disposable tampons is a device called The Keeper, made in Cincinnati, Ohio, which is a small, soft-rubber menstrual cup. This bell-shaped apparatus rests upside down near the bottom of the vagina, collecting menstrual fluid. Company owner Lou Crawford has been producing The Keeper since 1987. Its design is based on an early reusable rival to the tampon called the Tassett, which first appeared in the 1930s. Crawford, who was unable to use tampons herself, bought a Tassett in the late 1950s and used it "forever." When her daughter asked where she could buy one, Crawford checked and discovered the company had gone out of business in the early 1970s. Recognizing that this simple device was not only convenient but had environmental benefits too, she resurrected it four years ago as The Keeper.

We saw an advertisement for The Keeper in *Garbage* magazine; it's an innocuous little promotional piece that describes the product as a "menstrual" cup, includes a small photo of the device, notes it is "FDA accepted" (the FDA just accepts or rejects; it doesn't "approve" any product), has a life expectancy of at least ten years and costs $35.00 U.S. plus $2.00 shipping and handling. We were shocked to learn from Lou Crawford that not one, but several magazines have rejected this ad. Meanwhile, the throwaways are advertised *ad infinitum* and *ad nauseam*, without, of course, ever mentioning the word "menstrual." Maybe that's why The Keeper ad is regularly repudiated.

Finally, a few words about reusable baby diapers. They too have come a long way from the old days of huge cotton squares that required endless folding. Some parents have dubbed this new generation the "designer" diaper, no doubt because their creators were inspired by the sophisticated designs of their disposable competitors. The modern cloth diaper is shaped, has elasticized waist and leg openings and often comes with velcro or snap closings. Diaper service diapers, on the other hand, use the plain old cotton squares, but suggest that parents use breathable covers with velcro closings—reusable, of course—to keep everything in place.

Flannel seems to be the fabric of choice for the lining and exterior of most cloth diapers. For absorbency, layers of flannel, batting or both are sewn together. Some types allow for the addition of cotton liners that draw moisture away from the baby's skin and increase absorbency for night wear. A waterproof, breathable diaper cover is standard on most brands.

There are plenty of reasons to switch from disposable to reusable diapers and menstrual products. Certainly, the environmental issue is crucial. Production of throwaway paper products such as sanitary napkins and tampons not only wastes forest resources, it consumes nonrenewable petrochemicals, which in turn create excess wrapping, nonbiodegradable backings for pads and those perverse plastic applicators that torment waste treatment workers and beachcombers, and threaten seabirds and marine animals.

Then there are the traces of dioxins, furans and other organochlorines found in some chlorine-bleached products, which no one can prove do any real harm. But nobody will vouch for their complete safety either. We find this more than a little disquieting. When organochlorines get dumped into rivers, lakes and oceans, however, there is no question they do damage—not immediately, perhaps, but eventually, and the extent of this damage can't even be quantified. Some legacy we're leaving for our kids. And you'll save some money by using reusables. Send what you save to a good, active environmental group (maybe even ours) or to another worthy cause.

What follows is an incomplete list of the companies making reusable sanitary products. Because our population is aging rapidly, incontinence pads are another item for which there is growing demand; we have a few listings for these products too. We tried our best, but we're happy to say that cottage industries are springing up all over—it's impossible to keep up. (We do apologize for those we've missed, and if your company is in this category, write and let us know. We'll include you in the next edition.) If you live in a large town or city, you can also try health food stores, food co-ops and other "alternative" retail outlets for reusable menstrual products.

And, finally, if you're still skeptical, just keep an open mind. As one caller to a Vancouver radio phone-in show said recently, "I'm now doing things for the sake of the environment that I would never have dreamed of doing six months ago."

Harmony Naturwear (reusable sanitary pads, incontinence pads): 8 - 190 Allen Street East, Waterloo, Ontario, N2J 1K1

Many Moons (reusable sanitary pads): 14 - 130 Dallas Road, Victoria, British Columbia, V8V 1A3

Moon Pads (reusable sanitary pads): Tumamas Products, P.O. Box 166, Boulder Creek, CA, 95006

New Cycle (reusable sanitary pads): c/o Menstrual Health Foundation, P.O. Box 3248, Santa Rosa, CA, 95402

Saratech Inc. (a full line of reusable adult incontinence products and baby diapers): R.R. #3, King City, Ontario, L0G 1K0

Sisterly Works (sea sponges, reusable sanitary pads): R.R. #3, Box 107, Port Lavaca, Texas, 77979

The Keeper (reusable menstrual cup): Box 20023, Cincinnati, OH, 45220

Waddles in White (reusable diapers) and **We Care** (reusable sanitary pads): 28 Fairleigh Avenue South, Hamilton, Ontario, L8M 2K2

Women's Choice (reusable sanitary pads, incontinence pads): P.O Box 245, Gabriola, British Columbia, V0R 1X0

For other reusable diapers companies, check parenting magazines, and for diaper services, try your local Yellow Pages.

9

How British women
beat them on the bleaches

The idea for this book—and the campaign to pressure the North American sanitary protection industry to switch to more environmentally friendly products—is not our own. We like to give credit where it's due—the inspiration emerged from across the sea and the brilliant example set by the Women's Environmental Network (WEN) in Great Britain.

How did this small, but incredibly energetic, group of British women take on the small, but incredibly paternalistic, cluster of British sanitary protection companies and make them take notice of some serious shortcomings in their products? And then *do* something about them? Here's the story, as told by Bernadette Vallely, co-founder and director of WEN:

It all began during the summer of 1988 when I had dinner with some friends in North London. A few of them worked for Greenpeace, which had started a campaign about chlorine-bleached paper a few years earlier. They told me about the "Rip It Up!" Campaign organized by Greenpeace Sweden that encouraged members of the public to literally tear up product packaging to see what it was made of. Inside the brown or printed wrapping, they often found pure white paper, proof that the paper was chlorine-bleached. The public sent back packages in the thousands to manufacturers.

A few years after this campaign began, over 90 percent of Swedish consumer products were packaged in either chlorine-free or unbleached paper. This seemed to us such a promising and immediate form of consumer action that we began to discuss the merits of running a similar campaign in Great Britain. In the end we decided to focus on women's consumer products. Little did we know that this decision would unearth so much crucial information about the sanitary protection industry that it would never be the same again.

We spent nearly six months researching the project—going into libraries, looking up old files, consulting books and reports that had never seen the light of day. We wrote letters to all the sanitary protection companies, and mostly received standard replies. It was a real eye-opener. One company in Britain had a reputation for good relations with the public. I can remember as a schoolgirl writing to a "Sister Marion" for more information about menstruation and getting a nice personal reply with a free packet of sanitary napkins. For a young schoolgirl this is exciting, an easy way to get "hooked" on a company's product.

Well, ten of us wrote—all within a month—to the same "Sister." Imagine our surprise when we all got replies signed by ten different people! I suppose we were a bit naive to believe that there really was a "Sister" sitting at a desk answering all of our letters, but we started to treat the industry with a bit more suspicion after that.

By the winter of 1988, our research had grown into thousands of pages. We tried to find out everything about the paper industry, concentrating on diapers, sanitary napkins and tampons. We had to overcome the truly British embarrassment of looking into a very intimate product. We learned that manufacturers intentionally fostered this discomfort—it successfully enabled the industry to conceal information from women. The British industry had sold us secrecy, sterility and cleanliness all wrapped up together, and it perpetuated the patriarchal idea that we shouldn't discuss women's menstruation in public. It was very convenient for the companies.

We discussed numerous possibilities when we were doing our research, including selling unbleached sanitary products ourselves. At one point, we held secret discussions with a major chain interested in buying large quantities of unbleached sanitary napkins from abroad. I telephoned the managing director of one major company and asked him how I could buy a large quantity of unbleached napkins. I didn't tell him my real name or mention the environment. His answer astonished me: "Oh, you don't want to worry about dioxins, love. No one knows about them in this country!" He, apparently, knew all along.

Our determination to continue gathered strength from that day. We tried to find out everything about the industry we could. There wasn't room to put it all in our book, *The Sanitary Protection Scandal*; we soon ended up with filing cabinets full of paper.

We couldn't find out about tampons from our own sources here in Britain, but we got masses of information from the

United States. The toxic shock syndrome (TSS) scandal had not reached Britain the same way that it had in North America—we had to start educating women virtually from scratch. No labeling system telling women about the absorbency of tampons or about TSS was available in the U.K. To this day, the sanitary protection companies put only a cursory mention of the illness inside the box. They certainly don't include it in information they so generously hand out to school-aged girls just starting to use their products, even though these young consumers are the most at risk.

The Women's Environmental Network launched the Tampon Safety Campaign in the summer of 1990. Since then, five young women (that we know about) have died from TSS and almost a hundred more have suffered from long-term effects of the disease—effects that are never mentioned in the leaflets. Thousands more may have contracted TSS in its mildest form and never realized. Physicians are not required to report this disease in Britain, and we are campaigning to get basic information to the medical community as well as to users of tampons.

The Tampon Safety Campaign is spearheaded by the parents or loved ones of those who have died or suffered from TSS. The families are incredulous that such a simple-looking product could change their lives so very drastically. A WEN poster about TSS, entitled "Out of Sight, Out of Mind," is available for universities, schools, workplaces and public toilets. The poster hangs on the inside door of a toilet stall, a place where women can read the message in private without being interrupted. We've distributed many thousands of posters throughout the U.K.

When we launched our Campaign for Unbleached Paper on February 14, 1989, we had no idea of the response we would get. One disposable diaper company, Peaudouce, had decided a few weeks earlier to launch a chlorine-free diaper made entirely from a mechanical pulp. So the issue was already beginning to be news. Two weeks later, Procter & Gamble announced their "environmentally friendly" diaper which was oxygen-bleached. WEN took part in interviews about these developments and gave muted responses to the press, even though it was obvious that some companies were changing before our campaign launch.

It was funny to watch the diaper companies' press conferences. They announced they were changing to chlorine-free products, but they wouldn't say why. They knew if they said too much, they would risk launching an environmental campaign themselves, make other companies look stupid and worry mothers who had used their products previously. Rumor has it that the other companies were furious with Peaudouce for "breaking ranks" and buying chlorine-free pulp first. Apparently, the managing directors had a stand-up row that hasn't healed to this day.

Once our campaign began, the publicity about chlorine-free sanitary products escalated. We made a television program with *World in Action*, a major documentary series in Britain watched by about one in five people. After the half-hour show on sanitary products aired, viewers jammed the station switchboard with calls about the issue. The British Broadcasting Corporation televised a program on diapers when we held our initial press conference, and asked parents to call in and say if they agreed with our campaign. The question was simple: Do you want chlorine-free diapers? The astonished researcher at the office told me afterwards that ten thousand people had telephoned and about 98 percent said they wanted chlorine-free; the rest wanted more information. Our hunch was correct. Parents didn't really care what color their babies' diapers were. When they found out that "whiter-than-white" diapers caused environmental problems, they were very angry.

WEN received thousands of letters from the public asking about the issue of chlorine pulps. The U.K. Department of the Environment told us they received more letters from women on chlorine, paper and diapers than any other issue that year—even more than rain forests.

Within the first six weeks of launching the campaign against chlorine in paper, we were inundated with press and public inquiries. We had no money and no support other than from Greenpeace, which remains to this day a firm ally. Some other environment groups were scathing about our ability to pull off the campaign. One group told us that we wouldn't get any media attention, but they had to eat their words when we managed to get press coverage not just once or twice but several times—front pages, back pages and inside features in every major newspaper in the country. My favorite headline was, "We'll fight them on the bleaches, says an army of women." Journalists rang us up and told us we had the story of the year, and WEN received much acclaim for bringing the issue to the public's attention.

The companies reacted swiftly—most of them anyway. While tampon companies refused to meet us, discuss the issue or acknowledge any part in the environmental problem, the rest of the industry sought to clean up its act. Within six weeks of launching the campaign, WEN had assurances from all the manufacturers of sanitary napkins and diapers that they would no longer use chlorine to bleach their products. Some were able to turn to chlorine-free pulp immediately while others claimed supply difficulties and switched to oxygen-bleached pulp. They all produced labeling and advertising logos that proclaimed their products as "environmentally friendly."

Our campaign did not stop with sanitary napkins and diapers, however. Once the members of the public were aware of the issue of chlorine bleaching, they began to demand more chlorine-free products. Supermarkets and manufacturers responded with products ranging from coffee filters and toilet rolls to office copy paper and packaging.

In 1990, WEN carried out the first major survey of the paper industry: *Paper Mills in the UK: Environmental Impact Report*. Much to our surprise, the industry greeted this report with enthusiasm. The two main findings were: 65 percent of all mills had broken the law by discharging effluent into rivers or the sea in the previous eighteen months, and an astonishing 40 percent had switched from chlorine-bleached pulp to non-chlorine bleached or recycled pulps. By targeting a small corner of the industry, the Achilles' heel perhaps, we were able to educate both consumers and paper mills about the chlorine problem, and bring about a noticeable change in one of this country's biggest industries.

One interesting thing that happened while we were conducting the campaign was the change in style within the industry itself. Before we launched the campaign, many of the people we contacted refused to speak or answer questions.

We had to enlist the aid of an opposition Member of Parliament to help us at one point in our research. Of course, they responded to those letters, and this was a good source of information for us. Once we launched the campaign, many industry spokespeople told us in public: "You only needed to ask and we would have helped all along." We had asked, of course, as consumers and as members of the public, but they simply ignored us. They never realized we would actually run a campaign against them.

It did not take long for the industry to try bribery. One man actually phoned me—twenty-four hours before the launch of our book, *The Sanitary Protection Scandal*, and six hours before the *World in Action* television program—with this interesting proposition: "Okay, I have been given permission by a major Swedish paper company to ask you how much it would cost *not* to run your campaign in the United Kingdom." It was relatively easy to laugh when he asked me to name a figure.

The contrast between that behavior before the campaign and the "let's all talk together and be friends" attitude that we got after the campaign could not have been more stark. Companies who sent representatives to see us in our tiny offices on City Road (we've since moved to more spacious quarters) usually got a rough ride. We were honest and blunt, but we maintained a healthy and open relationship with many of them. We meet relatively frequently, moving along the debate each time, hoping always to get the disposable companies to stop trading and switch to reusable services!

Some companies—the tampon companies, especially—refuse to talk to us at all. They do not answer letters written by us individually or from the organization. It makes us feel they must have something to hide after all.

WEN in Britain has grown considerably since we launched our *Campaign for Unbleached Paper*. We now focus on four specific areas within the pulp and paper industry. We have a full-time information and scientific team, headed by our resident chemist, Ann Link, who works on dioxins, technology and chemicals. This team also covers new developments in issues about diaper services and breastfeeding. The other areas include our Tampon Safety, Forest and Packaging campaigns. We have fifteen full-time women and another half-dozen researchers and volunteers who come in more irregularly, along with full-time staff that includes fundraisers, information and local group coordinators and an international coordinator.

WEN has been represented in international forums using our chlorine-free campaign as a positive example of how we can empower women through consumer action. We have organized exhibitions, published books and magazines, run conferences and helped set up WEN groups in many countries around the world.

Our basic philosophy is—do it!

10
The power of one, the glory of many

So, with your help, "do it" we will.

Bernadette Valley of the Women's Environmental Network has, in our opinion, outlined a workable, wonderfully simple blueprint for environmental action by consumers of sanitary products. Better still, the women of WEN have proved their strategy really works. Duplicating their achievement here—getting rid of chlorine gas as a bleaching agent for feminine hygiene products—would be good for both women and the environment. Totally eliminating all chlorine compounds from these products would be even better, along with several other changes—to packaging, labeling and ingredients.

Women may not possess much of the world's wealth—men own 99 percent of all private property, in fact—but we certainly do most of the shopping. In both Canada and the United States, retail grocery associations say women make over 80 percent of the purchases, which is no big surprise really. Of course we don't need expensive market surveys to tell us that women are the exclusive consumers of tampons and sanitary pads. (Even when brothers, husbands or the kids are sent off to buy these on our behalf, it's always with strict instructions—sometimes even a note—to get the "right" brand.)

Because we have this complete stranglehold on the market, sanitary product manufacturers are extremely vulnerable to consumer pressure—but only if we choose to use our clout. Corporations are driven first and foremost by profit, and are remarkably responsive when their earnings are at risk. They know shareholders are watching every move. So it makes sense to vote with our dollars for better products every time we shop. This notion is not new but, as far as we know, in North America the focus has never been women's sanitary products. (We can also do a host of other things to force companies to change for the better, and that's what this chapter is all about.)

So despite this potentially enormous consumer power, why do the companies continue to have the upper hand? We think it's because old taboos die slowly. When Toronto environmental writer and broadcaster Marjorie Lamb was growing up in the 1960s in a small Saskatchewan farming community, women's sanitary products were kept in a back room of the local store, far from the eyes of patrons. When you wanted to buy "Kotex" (yes, that's what you asked for), you hung around the magazine rack self-consciously waiting for a female clerk to be free at the cash register, then hurried forward and made your request. Off went the clerk to the back room, where she slipped your bulky, unmentionable package into a brown paper bag, and brought it back to the front counter. You paid and quickly disappeared into the street. Heaven forbid that any male ever witnessed this clandestine transaction!

(Women under forty should understand that this *was* the way of the world twenty-five or so years ago, and not just in rural Saskatchewan.)

Sanitary pads and tampons had graduated to the open shelves by the 1970s, but a veil of silence still surrounds menstrual products, interrupted only briefly by the attention paid to the TSS "crisis" of 1980-81. We rarely discuss them at all, let alone say anything about the burden they impose on landfill sites, whether their "ingredients" are safe or how they could be made much more environmentally sound.

We *should* be talking. Considering how the AIDS crisis forced condoms and safe sex practices onto the public agenda, surely there's hope for "feminine hygiene" products.

We know the idea of actually discussing sanitary napkins, tampons and menstruation is inconceivable to some. Frankly, they weren't on our own list of top ten topics before we started this book. But breaking the silence has been fascinating, informative and not at all embarrassing. And while we've been deeply disturbed by some of the information we learned, we've laughed a lot too (especially as we contemplated a fashion show to parade some of the wilder patterns of reusable sanitary pads...)

Women of all ages willingly shared their experiences with menstruation and sanitary products. They talked at length about the whole range of concerns, from product preferences and safety, to environmental "friendliness" and disposability, and just about everything in between—cramps, PMS, most memorable/mortifying moments and so on.

It's hard to emphasize the importance of talking without sounding trite. Talking gave us courage. ("You mean you've

actually tried those reusable sanitary pads? And they work?")
And, if not courage, at least some good inside info. More
than one woman we talked to reported shorter, less painful
periods after switching from tampons to sanitary pads, for
example. And since, realistically, this book is probably not
going to crack the *New York Times* bestseller list, we need you
to pass the message along. Now if every woman talked with
just two more about this subject (and they talked with two
more), we'd have it made.

Speaking up is even more important. How are we going to
change the world if we don't tell the powers-that-be what we
want?

We also want this book to generate some good grassroots
action to change things for the better. Now that you're aware
of the environmental and health issues at stake here—persistent organochlorine pollution from bleaching pulp with
chlorine, toxic shock syndrome, plastic tampon applicators
(those infernal "beach whistles"), forest depletion, landfill
and sewage treatment disposal, even diaper rash—it's time for
action.

There is plenty that one person—you—can do to change
the status quo. Maybe you're skeptical about the power of
one. Does writing a letter to a politician or company president really make one iota of difference? Does it matter if you
phone a toll-free number to complain about misleading
advertising? Or tell a manufacturer you're boycotting his
product for something less environmentally risky?

The answer to all these questions is emphatically "Yes!" In a
recent magazine advertisement, Scott Paper credited letter-writ-
ing customers for its new line of unbleached and recycled

household tissue products. Customers asked and they received. Politicians from all parties agree that voters' opinions do make a difference, particularly if they're expressed in face-to-face conversations or in personal letters. (By the way, letters have much more clout than a string of signatures on a petition, although petitions are still better than nothing at all.) And manufacturers need to be told directly why you're unhappy with their brand—if they're smart, they'll do something about it. These actions all add up, and they make a difference. Countless women are changing the world with their small but outspoken acts of environmental kindness *and* their complaints.

That some women are practicing the "power of one"—acting on the premise that one person really can make a difference—has changed other women's lives forever. Bernadette Vallely is a good example. In addition to promoting positive change in the British sanitary protection industry, she and her colleagues in the Women's Environmental Network have inspired many others with their commitment and passion. Far too many women to name have made a profound impact as environmentalists, but here are a few anyway:

- Lois Gibbs who, in 1978, made the connection between her children's illnesses and the toxic dumpsite at the nearby Love Canal. Her neighborhood activism was the seed for the U.S.-based Clearinghouse for Hazardous Waste, which works with over seven thousand groups across the United States providing information on toxic materials and grassroot campaign strategies for those seeking assistance.
- Self-taught forester Wangari Maathai of Kenya whose Green Belt movement grew from the humble beginnings of

a backyard tree nursery. She eventually recruited fifty thousand women to plant ten million trees, reclaiming eroded land and increasing much-needed firewood supplies.

- Setsuko Yamazoto of Japan became alarmed in the mid-1970s when a major airport was scheduled to be built out over a rare blue coral reef. She successfully led a crusade to stop this megaproject and has since become one of Japan's most influential environmentalists and development critics.

Some women do bring science backgrounds to the environmental struggle—and their knowledge is a gold mine. But a great many are ordinary people who simply dive in and tackle problems when they realize no one else is taking action on important issues. These "citizen scientists" learn what they need to know as they go along—often dizzyingly complex stuff—and refuse to be daunted by the experts and specialists. They're not fooled or put off by Ph.D.s who are paid handsomely to protect the status quo.

Some women are born into activism. Environmentalist Elizabeth May, now spokesperson for the Canadian chapter of the Sierra Club, fought valiantly against forest spraying in Nova Scotia while she was still in law school. She tells the story of going Christmas shopping in New York City as a young girl with her mother, Stephanie May, a fervent peace and disarmament activist. One window of the posh Lord & Taylor clothing store displayed a not-so-perfect picture of peace on earth— Santa Claus riding a rocket. "This is Christmas," her mother protested to the store manager. "How can you have Santa Claus and a symbol of militarism in the window? Everyone is going to complain." "Madam," he replied, "You are the first to complain." Whereupon Stephanie turned to her young daughter and said, "Elizabeth, I want that on my tombstone: She was the first to complain."

We hope you'll be the first on your block to complain about chlorine-bleached sanitary products with all their plastic packaging and mysterious ingredients. (People have been complaining about disposable diapers for quite some time, and the message, at least in Canada, is getting through. Sales of reusables are flourishing and we're seeing a major revival of diaper services.)

It's okay if you don't want to become a full-time activist. You can still accomplish a great deal as a part-timer. The problems are serious—your contribution is desperately needed. Here are some things you can do:

- Reduce your own household paper consumption, if you haven't already. You really don't need paper towels or paper napkins, and certainly not paper cups or plates (even for a picnic). Try living without them for a few weeks. You'll find they're easy to give up altogether.

- If you do use these household paper products, try to purchase brands with 100 percent recycled content with as much post-consumer fiber as possible, at least 50 percent. (If the label just says "Made from 100 percent recycled paper," it may be a total scam. These products are often made from pulp leftovers and paper offcuts that were always "recycled," long before it became a selling point. Complain about this misinformation!) If post-consumer recycled products are not available, ask for ones that are totally unbleached.

- Vote with your dollars for the most environmentally friendly disposable sanitary pads, the "tree-saver" brands made with chlorine-free mechanical pulps lightened with hydrogen peroxide. Stay away from the whiter than white ones!

- Write a letter to the sanitary protection company that produces your brand of "feminine hygiene" product (if you haven't already switched to reusables). Say you'd prefer a product that has not been bleached or treated with any chlorine compound at any stage of production—no chlorine gas, no chlorine dioxide, no hypochlorite. Ask for a full list of its product "ingredients." Ask for a detailed response to your questions. Then copy your letter to your federal politician with a note asking for "zero discharge" regulations that will eliminate, among other things, chlorine compounds in all pulp bleaching processes. Send along a copy of your letter to us so we can quote you.

- Send back the excess packaging. Demand that your sanitary protection company eliminate all plastic wrappings. Why individually wrap a product that's not sterile in the first place?

- Switch to reusable sanitary products if you haven't already. (See page 140 for names and addresses of companies producing them.)

- Most sanitary product companies have toll-free (1-800) telephone numbers. (These numbers are listed in the back of this book on pages 164-165). Use this service to ask very specific questions about how each brand is manufactured. Find out about chlorine or chlorine dioxide bleaching. Don't be fooled when they say, "We use an oxygen process."

(And, while you're at it, ask how many women have upper management positions with these companies.)

- Talk to your friends, colleagues, sisters and kids about the "sanitary protection" issue—and mothers and grandmothers too, of course, because they've probably got some great stories to tell. Pass the message along about the environmental dangers of chlorine-bleached paper products. Talk about toxic shock syndrome.

- Demand more specific product labeling from manufacturers—ask for all the ingredients in tampons and sanitary napkins to be listed.

- If you are able to make recommendations about the type of paper you use at your office or at school, suggest 100 percent recycled stock, with plenty of post consumer content, unbleached stock, or chlorine-free paper (in that order). In fact, make the recommendation anyway, no matter what your position! And don't forget to recycle all this paper.

- Speak up!

- Join the WEED Foundation, sponsors of this book and project. Please send some money to help keep this campaign rolling along. (Here's the address so you won't have to hunt for it: Women & Environments Education and Development (WEED) Foundation, 736 Bathurst Street, Toronto, Ontario, M5S 2R4. Our phone number is 416-516-2600.) Or form your own nucleus of women committed to environmental change-for-the-better. While we most assuredly believe in the "power of one," we also know there's wonderful strength in numbers—the "glory of many."

And finally...

As this book was nearing completion, a letter arrived from Scott Paper in Vancouver. We had been impressed with Scott's new line of unbleached household tissue products—we thought that very little else had been sacrificed when whiter-than-white chlorine bleaching went by the wayside—and had asked for more information.

This letter was a fairly typical fence-sitting response, the kind we've come to expect from the industry, at least from those manufacturers still using chlorine. It defended pulp bleaching, and said that Scott's unbleached products weren't necessarily more environmentally sound than its bleached products. The company simply wanted to offer consumers a choice. (However, advertising copy for the new product line *does* mention that it's "more planet-friendly." You can't have it both ways.)

What interested us most, however, was the closing point: "A fact that you should understand is that if the Canadian sanitary tissue industry were to make nothing but unbleached products, the unbleached pulp required would be less than 5% of all the kraft pulp produced in the country."

This information was not news to us. We were aware from the beginning that women's sanitary products and diapers, together with household tissue products, constituted only a small fraction of the total paper consumed in North America. Implied in Scott's response, however, is the idea that even if this entire segment of the industry switches to unbleached, it won't make much difference.

Our position is that 5 percent is a whole lot better than nothing—especially when the same 5 percent adds up to tens of billions of single-use, non-recyclable paper products being dumped every year in Canada and the U.S. Greenpeace and other environment groups have been urging consumers to take action—and we as women can easily apply ourselves and our clout to the segment of the market we virtually own. At the same time, Scott is right that 5 percent *is* only the beginning, and we need to turn our attention to packaging, publishing, business, government and other major paper consumers. But first things first.

Where is government in all this? You may have noticed that we have not once mentioned the regulatory process or the role governments can and should play in stepping in to reduce or stop industrial pollution. When we began this project in June, 1990, Canadian government regulations on dioxin, furan and other organochlorine discharges from pulp mills were "imminent." A year and a half later when we finished this manuscript, the dioxin and furan regulations were finally announced. These regulations instruct bleached pulp mills to reduce dioxin and furan levels in their discharges to non-detectable levels. But still more waiting—the deadline for compliance is the beginning of 1994.

Environmental officials say that Canada is the first country in the world to bring down controls on dioxins and furans
in pulp mill effluents. They contend that these new limits,
coupled with other changes under federal fisheries legislation,
are a real boon to the environment.

But critics like Gord Perks, pulp and paper specialist for
Greenpeace in Toronto, argue that the new rules are too little, too late. "We're going from being a lot worse than
everybody else in the world to being a little bit worse."

Much of Perks' disappointment (and ours too) stems from
the government's decision to hold off on total organochlorine
controls. This comes just weeks after the release of a long-
awaited federal report which concluded that organochlorine
discharges from bleached pulp mills were "toxic" under environmental law. This federal report says that chlorinated
organic compounds from pulp bleaching are a hazard and
need to be reduced, although we go all the way and say it's
better to fully eliminate them. The government's decision
not to regulate this toxic effluent just strengthens our resolve
to stimulate change in other ways.

Well-motivated consumers can often get the job done faster
than governments, subject as politicians are to pressure and
browbeating from many sides, not least of all industry. We're not
asking the impossible, although the pulp and paper industry tries
to convince us otherwise. As we write, kraft and sulfite mills in
Sweden and Finland—and now the Port Mellon kraft mill in
British Columbia—are producing totally chlorine-free pulp. Part
of consumer action is pressing our governments to recognize
unbleached and chlorine-free paper products as better for the
environment and, yes, trying out those reusable alternatives.

One of the pulp and paper industry's standard comebacks to the toxic waste problem is that the life expectancy of humans hasn't suffered, that we're still living to grand old ages, maybe even longer than before. But look a little more closely at human health statistics. Sperm counts are down, the number of birth defects has doubled over the past twenty-five years, and Statistics Canada reports that the incidence of cancer has risen—according to current data, one in three of us will contract some form of the disease, and these statistics do not even include most skin cancers.

Life expectancy may not have suffered—at least not yet—but what about the *quality* of our lives, or our children's lives? Our own opinion is that, regarding health issues, North Americans are just beginning to reap what has been sown by the chemical industry and through chronic low doses of toxic compounds we receive through food, air and water, especially since the Second World War. Of course we're not blaming the pulp and paper industry for all of our health problems, but neither are we letting it off the hook. The sanitary protection companies must be more accountable for their products, both to women *and* the environment. Enough secrecy. A great deal can be done, but we have to wake up, and speak up for truly, healthy, sustainable alternatives.

Ever heard of the "boiled frog syndrome?" If you put a frog into a pot of cold water on the stove (so biologists say, and we'll take their word for it), and gradually heat up the water, you'll eventually make a disturbing observation. As the water slowly but surely rises toward the boiling point, the frog doesn't move a muscle, never tries to hop out of the pot. It never reacts at all to this gradual but grim change in its environment. It simply dies.

Are we smarter than the boiled frog? Can we escape the same fate?

This book—and your commitment—says that yes, we can. Let's begin.

APPENDIX: Major North American sanitary protection companies

CANADA

Cascades P.S.H. Inc.
999 Farrell Street
Drummondville, PQ
J2C 5P6
Toll-free #: 1-800-567-3842
Fax: (819) 477-8779
Products: Vania sanitary napkins,
pantyliners

Johnson & Johnson Inc.
P.O. Box 937, Station M
Montreal, PQ
H1V 9Z9
Toll-free #: 1-800-361-8068
Fax: (514) 251-4594
Products: Stayfree, Carefree, o.b.
tampons, Sure & Natural, Sure &
Natural Prima

Kimberly-Clark Canada Inc.
90 Burnhamthorpe Road West
Mississauga, ON
L5B 3Y5
No toll-free, long distance
customers can call (416) 277-
6755 collect
Phone: (416) 277-6550
Fax: (416) 277-6889
Products: Kotex pads, New
Freedom, Lightdays pantyliners

Playtex Ltd.
6363 Northam Drive
Malton, ON
L4V 1N5

No toll-free, long distance
customers can call (416)
677-6211 collect
Phone: (416) 677- 6211
Fax: (416) 677- 7965
Product: Playtex tampons

Procter & Gamble Inc.
P.O. Box 355, Station A
Toronto, ON
M5W 1C5
Toll-free #:1-800-668-0197
Fax: (416) 730-4122
Product: Always

Smith & Nephew Inc.
2100, 52e Avenue
Lachine, PQ
H8T 2Y5
Product: private label tampons for
retailers

Tambrands Canada Inc.
254 Consumers Road, Suite 280
Willowdale, ON
M2J 1R4
Toll-free #:1-800-268-3448
Fax: (416) 497-7188
Products: Tampax, Tampax
Compak, Maxithins

UNITED STATES

Johnson & Johnson,
Personal Products Co.
Van Liew Avenue
Milltown, NJ
08850
Toll-free # in the US: 1-800-
526-3967
Phone: (908) 524-0400

Kimberly-Clark Corp.,
Consumer Service
401 North Lake Street
Neenah, WI
45959
Toll-free # in the US: 1-800-
544-1847
Phone: (414) 721-2000
Fax: (414)721-6721

Playtex Family Products Corp.
215 College Road
Paramus, NJ '
07652
Toll-free # in the US: 1-800-
222-0453
Phone: (201) 265-8000

The Procter and Gamble Co.
#1 Procter and Gamble Plaza
Cincinnati, OH
45202
Toll-free # in the US: 1-800-
543-0480
Phone: (513) 983-1100
Fax : (513) 983-1828

Tambrands Inc.
777 Westchester Avenue
White Plains, New York
10604
Toll-free # in the US: 1-800-
523-0014
Phone: (914) 696-6000

Glossary

Acute toxicity: Toxic reaction that usually occurs shortly after exposure to a toxic agent (e.g., an effect that occurs within a few hours or days).

AOX (Adsorbable Organic Halogen): AOX is a measure of the halogen bound to organic matter and is usually expressed as kilograms per ton of air-dried pulp. Chlorine is one of five chemical elements known as halogens; the others are flourine, bromine, iodine and astatine. AOX can be used as a general indicator of the total amount of organochlorines discharged in pulp bleaching effluent.

Bioaccumulation: How an organism stores a higher concentration of a substance in its body than is found in the surrounding environment. For example, many organochlorines are fat-loving (lipophilic), and some accumulate in the fatty tissue of fish and mammals at levels that are frequently hundreds, thousands and even millions of times higher than the ambient water and air.

BOD (Biological Oxygen Demand): Wood pulping creates leftover fibers and organic particles. When a mill discharges these leftovers into a lake or stream, they begin to degrade, helped by bacteria. BOD is a measure of the dissolved oxygen taken from the surrounding water when this breakdown occurs. It can have an impact on aquatic life, which depends on dissolved oxygen for survival.

Carcinogen: Cancer-causing substance.

Chemi-Thermo-Mechanical Pulp (CTMP): A process that uses mechanical means such as grinders or refiners, assisted by some chemicals and heat, to break wood down into a pulp. Hydrogen peroxide rather than chlorine-based chemicals are used to lighten mechanical pulp to a cream color, if desired.

Chlorine: Yellow-green gas with a pungent odor, also called "elemental chlorine." Pulp mills use chlorine to delignify and bleach wood pulp to a high brightness ("whiter than white"). During the bleaching process, chlorine reacts and combines with organic material from the wood, producing a wide variety of "organochlorines" (up to a thousand or more), also known as "chlorinated organic matter."

Chlorine dioxide: A compound containing chlorine and oxygen. If chlorine dioxide is used to bleach pulp in place of chlorine gas, emissions of organochlorines are reduced, particularly the heavily chlorinated compounds (including some chlorophenols) as well as dioxins and furans.

Chlorine-free: Wood pulp that has been bleached without chlorine gas. However, other chlorine compounds, such as chlorine dioxide and hypochlorite, are often used to make "chlorine-free" bleached pulp. Truly chlorine-free pulps are now designated "chlorine-compound free."

Chronic toxicity: Toxic effects that occur weeks, months or even years after exposure to a toxic agent, or as a result of long-term, low-level exposure.

Dioxins: Chlorinated compounds that are unwanted byproducts of processes using chlorine, such as pulp bleaching and burning of chlorinated compounds—copper smelting, combustion of leaded gasoline, municipal waste incineration, production of pesticides, etc. The dioxins are a family of 75 related compounds, the most toxic being 2,3,7,8- tetrachlorodibenzo-p-dioxin (2,3,7,8-TCDD).

Effluent: Waste material discharged into the environment.

Furans: A family of 135 chlorinated compounds, the most potent being 2,3,7,8-tetrachorodibenzo-p-furan (2,3,7,8-TCDF).

Hydrogen peroxide: Used to lighten wood pulp by making the brown lignin colorless. Hydrogen peroxide breaks down into hydrogen and oxygen, making it possibly the most environmentally benign chemical used by the pulp and paper industry. It also removes toxic resin acids from pulp.

Hydrophobic: "Water-hating." Most organochlorines are not readily soluble in water. Instead they gravitate toward fatty tissue in living organisms.

Kraft pulping: Also known as sulfate pulping, this is the most common wood pulping process. Wood is "cooked" in several stages in sulfur-based and caustic solutions to separate the glue-like lignin from the long, white cellulose fibers that are the key ingredient in pulp and paper products. Bleaching this pulp further with chlorine to create bright white pulp results in the formation of organochlorines, including dioxins and furans. Kraft pulp is one of two chemically derived pulps, the other being sulfite.

Lignin: Natural resinous glue in wood. It is removed and/or bleached out during chemical pulping (kraft or sulfite) processes, but most of it remains as part of the finished pulp in mechanical pulping processes, such as CTMP.

Lipophilic: "Fat-loving." Substances that tend to be absorbed into fat or oil, including the fatty tissue of humans, animals and plants.

Mechanical pulping: Physically grinding raw wood to a pulp—many variations of mechanical pulping, including CTMP, RMP (Refiner Mechanical Pulping), TMP (Thermo-Mechanical Pulping) and BCTMP (Bleached Chemi-Thermo-Mechanical Pulping). Also called the alphabet pulps for obvious reasons!

Mutagen: Any substance that damages genes and causes inherited disorders.

Organic compounds: Compounds made from carbon and hydrogen—the building blocks of life. Most naturally occurring organic compounds are readily biodegradable. When they are synthetically combined with other materials, such as chlorine, they may become persistent and toxic.

Organochlorine: An organic compound containing some chlorine. Organochlorines are unwanted byproducts of chemical pulp bleaching in which chlorine and chlorine-based compounds have been used. Thousands of chlorinated organic compounds have been created for a variety of applications, including pesticides, industrial solvents, deodorants, disinfectants, refrigerants, etc. Only a small proportion of the organochlorines created when wood pulp is bleached with chlorine-based chemicals has been identified.

Oxygen bleaching: Also called "oxygen delignification." An early stage in the pulping process during which oxygen is used to remove some of the glue-like lignin from the raw wood, before the pulp is bleached with chlorine compounds.

Persistent: Chemicals that remain in the environment and do not degrade or metabolize into harmless constituents for months, years or even decades.

Primary treatment: A crude type of treatment for wood pulp effluents. Essentially a filtering/settling-out process for solid matter such as bark fragments and wood fiber.

Secondary treatment: Treatment of mill waste using microbes to break down organic constitutents of the effluent. Most secondary treatment processes reduce the acute toxicity of the waste, but may be less effective in reducing the chronic toxicity.

Sulfite pulping: A chemical pulping process, much like sulfate (kraft) pulping, but much less widely used. It also produces unwanted organochlorines if the pulp is bleached with chlorine-based compounds.

Ton: Also known as a short ton, it weighs 2,000 pounds. One ton equals 0.9072 of a tonne (or metric ton).

Tonne: A metric ton. Weighs 1,000 kilograms or about 2,204 pounds. One tonne equals 1.1023 tons.

Toxicity: Harmful effects produced by exposure to a substance.

Toxic shock syndrome (TSS): Serious, sometimes fatal, illness strongly linked to tampon use. Symptoms include high temperature, vomiting and diarrhea, headache, sore throat, aching muscles, sunburn-like rash and rapid drop in blood pressure.

Sources

Introduction

Costello, Alison, et al. *The Sanitary Protection Scandal*. London: The Women's Environmental Network, 1989.

"Cutting CO_2 with Saplings and Slogans." *Garbage, The Practical Journal for the Environment* Vol. 2, No. 6 (November/December 1990): p. 80.

Durning, Alan. "How Much Is 'Enough?'" *World•Watch* Vol. 3, No. 6 (November/December, 1990): p. 12.

Grocery Attitudes of Canadians 1991. A survey conducted for the Grocery Products Manufacturers of Canada by Dialogue Canada. Toronto: 1991.

Warwick, Baker & Fiore. "How Concerned Are Consumers Over Factors Affecting The Environment?" New York: May, 1990.

Chapter 1
Chlorine: The curse of bright white paper

Allard, A.S., et al. "Environmental Fate of Chloroguaiacols and Chlorocatechols." *Water Science & Technology* Vol. 20, No. 2 (1988): pp. 131-41.

Andersson, T., and Forlin, Lars. "Physiological Disturbances in Fish Living in Coastal Water Polluted with Bleached Kraft Pulp Mill Effluents." *Canadian Journal of Fisheries and Aquatic Sciences* Vol. 45 (1988): pp. 1525-36.

Bertell, Rosalie. International Institute of Concern for Public Health, Toronto. From a speech entitled "Scientific Concerns for the Future Survival of the Human Race" presented to the

Canadian Wholesale Drug Association, January 23, 1991.

Boddington, M.J., et al. *Priority Substances List Assessment Report No. 1: Polychlorinated Dibenzodioxins and Polychlorinated Dibenzofurans.* Prepared for Environment Canada and Health and Welfare Canada. Ottawa: Supply and Services Canada, 1990.

Canadian Pulp and Paper Association. Various brochures. Montreal.

Carson, Rachel. *Silent Spring.* (Twenty-fifth anniversary edition). Boston: Houghton Mifflin Company, 1987.

The Chlorine Institute, Washington

Collishaw, N., and Leahy, K. "Mortality Attributable to Tobacco Use in Canada, 1989." *Chronic Diseases in Canada* Vol. 12, No. 4 (July/August, 1991): pp. 46-9.

Colodey, A.G., et al. "Effects of Pulp and Paper Mill Effluents on Estuarine and Marine Environments in Canada: A Brief Review." Paper presented at the 17th Toxicity Workshop, November, 1990. Vancouver, British Columbia.

Colodey, A.G., and Sinclair, W.F. "An Economic, Technical and Biological Review of the British Columbia Council and Forest Industries (COFI) Report: Sustainable Development and the B.C. Pulp and Paper Industry (March, 1990)," *Regional Review Report 90-1.* Unpublished report for Environment Canada (June, 1990, as amended February, 1991).

Craig, G., et al. "Toxicity and bioaccumulation of AOX and EOX." *Pulp & Paper Canada* Vol. 91 (1990): pp. 39-45.

Dioxin/Organochlorine Center, Eugene, Oregon, and the Environmental Law Clinic, University of Oregon, Eugene, Oregon.

The Encyclopedia Britannica. 15th edition, Chicago: 1988.

Environment Canada. "Dioxins in Sediments Study Release." (News Release). April 5, 1991.

Eysenbach, E.J., et al. "Pulping effluents in the aquatic environment." *Tappi Journal* Vol. 73, No. 8 (August, 1990): pp. 104-6.

Fleming, Bruce. Researcher, PAPRICAN, Montreal, Personal communication. Spring, 1991.

Great Lakes Science Advisory Board. *1991 Report to the International Joint Commission.* September, 1991.

Hallett, D. President, Eco Logic, Rockwood, Ontario. Personal communication. Summer, 1991.

Jacobson, J.L., et al. "Effects of exposure to PCBs and related compounds on growth and activity in children." *Journal of Toxicology and Teratology* Vol. 12 (1990): pp. 319-26.

————. "Effects of in utero exposure to polychlorinated biphenyls and related contaminants on cognitive functioning in young children." *Journal of Pediatrics* Vol. 116 (1990): pp. 38-45.

Jones, Sheila, et al. *Effluents from Pulp Mills Using Bleaching: Priority Substances List Assessment Report No. 2.* Prepared for Environment Canada and Health and Welfare Canada. Ottawa: Supply and Services Canada, 1991.

Kroesa, Renate. *The Greenpeace Guide to Paper.* Vancouver: Greenpeace, 1990.

Lindstrom-Seppa, P., and Oikari, A. "Biotransformation and other toxicological and physiological responses in rainbow trout caged in a lake receiving effluents of pulp and paper industry." *Aquatic Toxicology* Vol. 16 (1990): pp. 187-204.

Mehrle, P.M, et al. "Toxicity and Bioconcentration of 2,3,7,8-Tetrachlorodibenzodioxin and 2,3,7,8-Tetrachlorodibenzofuran in Rainbow Trout." *Environmental Toxicology and Chemistry* Vol. 7 (1988): pp. 47-62.

Mittelstaedt, Martin. "The Case Against Chlorine." *The Globe and Mail*, August 31, 1991.

National Council of the Paper Industry for Air and Stream Improvement (NCASI). "Effects of Biologically Treated Bleached Kraft Mill Effluent on Cold Water Stream Productivity in Experimental Stream Channels." *Technical Bulletin No. 566*, Fifth Progress Series. 1989.

Paasiverta, J. "Organochlorine compounds in the environment." *Water Sciences & Technology* Vol. 20, No. 2 (1988): pp. 119-29.

Paper Industry Information Office (U.S.). Dioxin Fact Sheet. Sent via Fraser Company, Edmunston, New Brunswick.

"Proposed mill presents an unacceptable risk." *The Globe and Mail*, March 6, 1990, p. A7.

Rainey, Margaret, and Kroesa, Renate. "Pulp Mill Effluent Effects: A Compilation of Recent Swedish Studies." Unpublished report for Greenpeace. May, 1991.

Sprague, J.B., and Colodey, A.G. "Toxicity to Aquatic Organisims of Organochlorine Substances in Kraft Mill Effluents." Unpublished report for Environment Canada, IP-100. (June, 1989).

Stewart, Alistair. Pulp & Paper Coordinator, Municipal-Industrial Strategy for Abatement (MISA), Environment Ontario. Personal communication. Spring, 1991.

Swain, W.R. "Human health consequences of consumption of fish contaminated with organochlorine compounds." *Aquatic Toxicology* Vol. 11 (1988): pp. 357-77.

Swain, W.R., Eco Logic, Ann Arbor, Michigan. Testimony before the Alberta-Pacific Environment Impact Assessment Review Board, Public Hearing Proceedings, Vol. 43. Edmonton, Alberta. December 4, 1989.

Taylor, L. "Pulp mill toxin levels broaden shellfish ban." *Vancouver Sun*, June 15, 1989, p. A14.

Thornton, Joe. *The Product is the Poison, Part I: The Case for a Chlorine Phase-out*. Washington: Greenpeace, 1991.

Vallentyne, Jack. *The Case for Phasing Out Organohalogens*, Canada Centre for Inland Waters, distributed by Greenpeace, Toronto.

Van Strum, C., and Merrell, P. *No Margin of Safety: A Preliminary Report on Dioxin Pollution and the Need for Emergency Action in the Pulp and Paper Industry*. Washington: Greenpeace, 1987.

Von Stackelberg, P. "Whitewash, The Dioxin Cover-up." *Greenpeace Magazine* (March/April, 1989): pp. 6-11.

Webster, T. "Why Dioxin and Other Halogenated Aromatic Hydrocarbons are Bad News." *Journal of Pesticide Reform* Vol. 9 (Winter, 1990): p. 32.

Chapter 2
Pulp, paper and other consuming passions

American Paper Institute. Various brochures. New York.

Angus Reid Group. "Consumers continue to express strong willingness to make financial sacrifices for the environment." *The Reid Report* Vol. 5, No. 10 (November/December, 1990).

Bonsor, N., McCubbin, N., and Sprague, J. *Kraft Mill Effluents in Ontario*. Expert Committee on Kraft Mill Toxicity. Toronto: Queen's Printer, 1989.

Colodey, A.G. "Environmental Impact of Bleached Pulp and Paper Mill Effluents in Sweden, Finland, and Norway: Implications to the Canadian Environment." Discussion paper. Unpublished report for Environment Canada. June, 1989.

Colodey, A.G., et al. "Effects of pulp and paper mill effluents on estuarine and marine environments in Canada: A brief review." Paper presented at the 17th Annual Toxicity Workshop, November, 1990, Vancouver, British Columbia.

DeBonis, Jeff. Willamette National Forest Timber Sale Planner. Open letter to Dale Robertson, chief of the U.S. Forest Service. *The Inner Voice* (newsletter of the Association of Forest Service Employees for Environmental Ethics). Eugene, Oregon. Summer, 1989.

Environment Ontario. *Interim Pollution Reduction Strategy for Ontario Kraft Mills*. Toronto: Queen's Printer. April, 1989.

Environment Ontario. *Preliminary report on the first six months of process effluent monitoring in the MISA pulp and paper sector.* Toronto: Queen's Printer, 1991.

Floegel, Mark. Greenpeace U.S.A. Personal communication. Spring and fall, 1991.

Forestry Canada. *The State of Forestry in Canada.* Ottawa: Minister of Supply and Services, 1991.

"Fortune 500 List of Largest U.S. Industrial Corporations." *Fortune.* April 22, 1991: pp. 286-304.

Gaudette, Pierre. Canadian Pacific Forest Products, Technical Services Manager. Personal communication. Spring, 1991.

Greenpeace Sweden. Internal communication (update). Chlorine-free kraft pulp capacity in Sweden as of May, 1991.

Hanson, J.P. "Recofluff: Can Recycled Fibre Deflect Consumer Hostility?" *Nonwovens Industry.* March, 1991.

Hart, Howard. President, Canadian Pulp and Paper Association. Introduction to "From the Forests of Canada to the Markets of the World." Brochure. Montreal: Canadian Pulp and Paper Association, 1990: p. 3.

Hillyer, Ann. Staff lawyer, West Coast Environmental Law Association. Personal communication. Spring, 1991.

Klinkenberg, Rose. "Witches' Brew." *Nature Canada* (Summer, 1989): pp. 10-11.

Kroesa, Renate. Chemist, Greenpeace Vancouver. Personal communication. Spring, 1991.

———. *The Greenpeace Guide to Paper.* Vancouver: Greenpeace, 1990.

———. "Sustainable Paper Production: Specific Actions for Environmental Compatibility." A paper presented to "Revolution or Evolution," Pulp and Paper International Symposium, Leningrad. April, 1991.

Maser, Chris. "Voices in the Forest." From *The Nature of Things* with David Suzuki, (television series). Canadian Broadcasting Corporation. Toronto: 1991.

McCrory, Colleen. Valhalla Society, Personal communication. Spring and fall, 1991

McKay, Paul. "An Industry at the Crossroads." *Toronto Star*, Nov. 27, 1990.

"The mill that won't ruin rivers." *British Columbia Report.* (May 28, 1990): p. 27.

Mittelstaedt, Martin. "Cleanup program for fish fails in Lake Superior." *The Globe and Mail*, January 24, 1991, p. A4.

Myres, Anthony. Health and Welfare Canada, Environmental

Substances Division, Priority Substances Section. Personal communication. Spring, 1991.

The Native Forest Council. "Stop the Chainsaw Massacre." Brochure. Eugene, Oregon.

Paasivirta, J., et al. "Organic chlorine compounds in lake sediments, III-Chlorohydrocarbons, free and chemically bound chlorophenols." *Chemosphere* Vol. 21 (1990): pp. 1355-70.

Procter & Gamble, Swalback Technical Centre, "Production of Pulp Disposable Diapers: Background and Environmental Considerations." Unpublished report. 1989.

Rainey, Margaret. Greenpeace Sweden. Personal communication. Spring, 1991.

Reeve, D.W., and Earl, P.F. "Chlorinated organic matter in bleached chemical pulp production. Part I: environmental impact and regulation of effluents." *Pulp & Paper Canada* Vol. 90, No. 4 (1989): pp. 128-32.

Ryan, John C. "Timber's Last Stand." *World•Watch* Vol. 3, No. 4 (July/August, 1990): pp. 27-34. Also personal communication and letter. Winter, 1991.

Sinclair, William. "Controlling Pollution From Canadian Pulp and Paper Manufacturers: A Federal Perspective." Ottawa: Environment Canada. July, 1988.

———. "Controlling Effluent Discharges from Canadian Pulp and Paper Manufacturers." *Canadian Public Policy* Vol. 17, No. 1 (1991): pp. 86-105.

Sprague, J.B., and Colodey, A.G. "Toxicity to Aquatic Organisms of Organochlorine Substances in Kraft Mill Effluents." Unpublished report for Environment Canada, IP-100, June 30, 1989.

Starke, Linda, et al. *State of the World 1991, A Worldwatch Institute Report on Progress Toward a Sustainable Society.* New York: W.W. Norton & Company, 1991.

Swift, Jamie. "The Growing Controversy Over Kraft-Mill Pollution." *Harrowsmith* Vol. 14, No. 5 (January/February, 1990): pp. 34-45.

West Coast Environmental Law Association. Newsletter, Vol. 15, December 21, 1990.

Chapter 3
Sanitary napkins: Padding the bottom line

Cain, Lydia. "End Uses for Nonwovens in 1989: What's Hot, What's Not." *Nonwovens World* (January/February, 1989): pp. 36-9.

Champagne, Anne. Staff environmentalist, Federation of Ontario

Naturalists. Personal communication. Spring, 1991.

Cook, Julie. Women's Environmental Network, Tampon safety campaigner. Personal communication. Spring, 1990.

Cooke, C., and Dworkin, S. *The Ms. Guide to a Woman's Health*. New York: Doubleday, 1979.

Cornell, Camilla. " 'Natural' sanitary pad elicits naturalist critique." *Now*. Toronto: March 21-7, 1991.

Costello, Alison, et al. *The Sanitary Protection Scandal*. London: Women's Environmental Network, 1989.

Darby, Dennis. Procter & Gamble, Manager, Environmental, Professional and Regulatory Services, Personal communication. Toronto. Spring, 1991.

Delaney, J., et al. *The Curse: A Cultural History of Menstruation*. Revised edition. Urbana, Illinois: University of Illinois Press, 1988.

Dunn, Kate. "Government awaits test results on dioxin paper products." Montreal *Gazette*, December 8, 1987, p. C1.

Ferguson, Jock. "Dioxin found in Canadian paper products." *The Globe and Mail*, December 8, 1987, p. A13.

Gammie, Craig. Kimberly-Clark, Canada, Government Affairs—Environmental. Personal communication. Spring, 1991.

Goard, G. Pierre. "Peat moss sanitary pads launched." *The Globe and Mail*, March 12, 1991.

Health Products Task Force, City of Toronto, Department of Health. *Women's Health Products Study*. 1982.

Hoffman, Joda. Melitta, Cherry Hill, New Jersey. Personal communication. Spring, 1991.

Johnson & Johnson Inc. *Annual Report*. New Brunswick, New Jersey: 1990.

————. News release (describing launch of Sure & Natural Prima pad). Montreal, 1991.

Kimberly-Clark Corp. Form 10K, submitted to the U.S. Securities Commission, 1990.

Kleppe, J. "Feminine Hygiene: A Market Shifts Gears." *Nonwovens World* (June/July, 1990: pp. 33-4.

Kroesa, Renate. *The Greenpeace Guide to Paper*. Vancouver: Greenpeace, 1990.

Lamb, Marjorie. *Two Minutes a Day for a Greener Planet*. Toronto: HarperCollins Publishers Ltd: 1990.

Lavigne, Ghislaine. Johnson & Johnson Inc. Project leader, Public Affairs, Montreal. Personal communication. Spring, 1991.

National Council of the Paper Industry for Air and Stream Improvement (NCASI). "Assessment of Potential Health Risks From Dermal Exposure to Dioxin in Paper Products." *Technical Bulletin No. 534.* November, 1987.

Newhook, Ronald. Health and Welfare Canada, Environmental Substances Division, Priority Substances Section. Personal communication. Spring, 1991.

Petersen, Laurie. "Did You Think We Wouldn't Notice?" *Adweek's Marketing Week* (March 18, 1991).

"Private Label Feminine Hygiene: Fourth in the Sanpro Race." *Nonwovens Industry* (January, 1991): p. 50-1.

"Private Label Sanitary Sales Performed Well in 1989." *Nonwovens Industry* (January, 1990): pp. 48-50.

The Procter & Gamble Company. *Annual Report.* Cincinnati: 1990.

————. "Periods and Puberty: a practical guide for girls." Booklet. 1987.

Raloff, Janet. "Dioxin: Paper's Trace." *Science News* Vol. 135, No. 7 (February 18, 1989): pp. 104-6.

Simons Strategic Services Division. "Pulp and Paper Options for Northern Tasmania: Focus on Fibre, Markets and Technology Related to Non-Chlorine Bleaching." Prepared for the Government of Tasmania. Vol. 1 (June 8, 1990).

Smith, Eva. Deputy undersecretary, Swedish Ministry of the Environment. Personal communication. Spring, 1991.

Swift, Jamie. "The Growing Controversy Over Kraft-Mill Pollution." *Harrowsmith* Vol. 14, No. 5 (January/February, 1990): pp. 34-5.

Wolfe, Phyllis. New York Consumer Affairs, Personal Products, Johnson & Johnson. Letter to Judy Braiman-Lipson, Empire State Consumer Association, August 4, 1987.

Yin, Lillian. Food and Drug Administration, Ob-Gyn-Dental Devices Branch, Washington. Personal communication. Spring, 1991.

Chapter 4
Disposable diapers: A rash of misinformation

Alexander, Vanessa. "Time for a Change." *Probe Post* Vol. 12 (Spring, 1989): pp. 1-12.

Amer, Elizabeth. Councillor, City of Toronto. Personal communication. Spring, 1991.

Becker, Pauline, et al. "Alternatives in Diapering." Non-profit booklet distributed to hospitals, health units, etc. Camrose, Alberta: 1989.

Braiman-Lipson, Judy. President, Empire State Consumer Association, Rochester, New York. Personal communication. Spring, 1991.

Center for Policy Alternatives. "Update on Diapers—Revised: Eighteen Billion Disposable Diapers Thrown Away Every Year: A Summary of Recent Waste Reduction Activities by State and Localities." Washington: September, 1990.

City of Waterloo Recycling Committee. "Diaper Options." Brochure. 1990.

Darby, Dennis. Procter & Gamble Inc., Toronto Manager, Environmental, Professional and Regulatory Services. Personal communication. Spring, 1991.

Ellis, Olga. Wellesley Hospital, Toronto, Manager, Linen Services Dept. Personal communication. Spring, 1991.

Environment Canada. CSA Guidelines for Cloth Diapers (EcoLogo ECP-14-89). March 14, 1991.

———. CSA Guidelines for Diaper Services (Ecologo ECP-21-90). March 14, 1991.

Federation of Canadian Municipalities."Municipalities Demand Promises from Federal Leaders to Reduce Packaging." Policy statement. November 7, 1988.

"Fluff pulp prices trend down, but not sharply; consumption rises moderately." *Pulp & Paper Week* (December 3, 1990).

Franke, I. M. "Approach of a multinational company to assist management of solid waste—a research program for baby diapers." *INDA Journal* Vol. 3, No. 1: pp. 41-3.

Franklin, William. President, Franklin and Associates Ltd., Prairie Village, Kansas. Speech to diaper seminar, Toronto. Spring, 1991.

Franklin and Associates Ltd. "Energy and Environmental Profile Analysis of Children's Disposable and Cloth Diapers." Prairie Village, Kansas: July, 1990.

Freeman, Laurie. "Procter & Gamble." *Advertising Age* (January 29, 1991): pp. 16-17.

Gammie, Craig. Kimberly-Clark Canada, Government Affairs— Environmental. Personal communication. Spring, 1991.

Hanson, John. Executive Director, Recycling Council of Ontario. Personal communication. Spring, 1991.

Hibler, Michelle. "Cloth diapers." *Canadian Consumer* No. 7 & 8 (1990): pp. 23-7.

Hills, Paula. "Will Disposables Waste Away?" *Nonwovens World* (August, 1990): p. 10.

Holmes, Hannah. Contributing editor, *Garbage: The Practical Journal for the Environment*. Personal communication. Spring, 1991.

Holusha, John. "The Packaging Industry's New Fancy—Composting Garbage." *The New York Times*, February 24, 1991.

Hoornweg, Dan. Former Waste Management Coordinator, City of Guelph. Personal communication. Spring, 1991.

Kendall, P.R.W. Medical Officer of Health, City of Toronto. "Memorandum on the Health Implications of Using Cloth Diapers in Daycare Centres and Hospitals, to the Board of Health, City of Toronto." March 14, 1991.

The Landbank Consultancy Ltd. "A Review of Procter & Gamble's Environmental Balances for Disposable and Re-usable Nappies." Report prepared for the Women's Environmental Network. London: July, 1991.

Lehrburger, Carl. "Diapers: A Waste Management Perspective." *Nonwovens World* (February, 1990): pp. 18-21.

———. "Diapers: Environmental Impacts and Lifecycle Analysis." Report to the National Association of Diaper Services (NADS). January, 1991.

———. "The disposable diaper myth." *Whole Earth Review*. (Fall 1988): pp. 61-7.

Little, Arthur D. "Disposable versus Reusable Diapers: Health, Environmental and Economic Comparisons." Report to Procter & Gamble. Cambridge, Massachusetts, March 16, 1990.

Marbeck Resource Consultants. "Briefing Note on Diaper Services." Prepared for Environment Canada, Environmental Choice Program. November 21, 1989.

———. "Briefing Note on the Environmental Impacts of Cloth vs. Disposable Diapers." Prepared for Environment Canada, Environmental Choice Program, November 15, 1989.

McRobert, David. Former researcher, Pollution Probe, Toronto. Personal communication. Spring, 1991.

Minion, Kate. Procter & Gamble U.K., Communications Manager, Environmental Affairs. Letter. March 13, 1991.

Picard, Jerry. Ottawa Diaper Service, Plant Manager. Personal communication. Spring, 1991.

Pickup, Carol. Councillor, Municipality of Saanich. Personal communication. Spring, 1991.

"Procter & Gamble Exposed." *The Women's Environmental Network Newsletter* No. 19 (Autumn, 1991): p. 1, 3.

Procter & Gamble Inc. "Disposable diapers and the environment." Brochure.

———. Information package on municipal solid waste composting, paper diaper initiatives, and solid waste management.

Salzman, Jack. "Difficult Road Ahead for U.S. Diaper Industry." *Nonwovens World* (January, 1990): pp. 36-8.

Simmons, Ralph. "Disposability Highlights U.S. Legislative Agendas." *Nonwovens World* (March/April, 1990): p. 68.

Simoni, Suzanne. Recycling Council of Ontario, volunteer. Personal communication. Spring, 1991.

Solomon, Jolie. "Superabsorbent Diapers: Marketers Seek Doctors' Support Amid Health Concerns." *The Wall Street Journal*, May 9, 1986.

State of Wisconsin, Act 335, (1991).

Tambrands Inc. *Annual Report*. Lake Success, New York: 1990.

Tryens, Jeffrey. Center for Policy Alternatives, Washington. Personal communication. Spring, 1991.

"U.S. Disposal Problems on the Rise, Alternative Methods Pursued." *Nonwovens World* (March, 1989): pp. 34-5.

"Vying for Global Market Share." *Nonwovens World* (November/December, 1990): pp. 28-30.

Wilson, Jane. "Disposable Diapers." *Canadian Consumer* (August/September, 1987).

Women's Environmental Network. "Memorandum to the Advertising Standards Authority from the Women's Environmental Network: Pampers and the Environment." London: July, 1991.

Wright, Mark. "The Diaper Dilemma: Conscience Over Convenience." *Recover* (Winter 1990-1): pp. 20-4.

Chapter 5
Tampons, part one: The big flush

Addison, Geoff. R.V. Anderson Associates, Toronto. Personal communication. Spring, 1991.

Arvisais, Y. Health and Welfare Canada, Access to Information and Privacy Centre. Letter regarding problem reports for menstrual tampons sent to the Adverse Device Experience Network. June 3, 1991.

Barrett, K., et al. "Tampon-induced vaginal or cervical ulceration." *American Journal of Obstetrics Gynecology* (February, 1972): pp. 332-3.

Butler, Ishbel. Clean Ocean Committee, Maritime Fishermen's Union, Pictou, Nova Scotia. Personal communication. Spring, 1991.

Cain, Lydia. "End Uses for Nonwovens in 1989: What's Hot, What's Not." *Nonwovens World* (January/February, 1989): pp. 36-9.

Chanter, Bruce. Member, Harbour Clean-up Committee, Halifax. Personal communication. Spring, 1991.

Cochrane, Susan. Former Vice-President of Marketing, Tambrands Canada. Personal communication. Spring, 1991.

Costello, Alison, et al. *The Sanitary Protection Scandal.* London: Women's Environmental Network, 1989.

Critchley, Jay. Artist, Cape Cod, Massachusetts. Personal communication. Spring, 1991.

Delaney, J., et al. *The Curse: A Cultural History of Menstruation.* Revised edition. Urbana, Illinois: University of Illinois Press, 1988.

Dribben, M. "Cleaning Liberty's Shore." *Bergen Record,* July 2, 1986.

Eaton, Peter. Environment Canada, Halifax, Environmental Protection, Head of Quality Evaluation Section. Personal communication. Spring, 1991.

Field Operations Directorate, Health and Welfare Canada. "Problem Report—Medical Devices [tampons]." Spring, 1991.

Fox, H. "The pathology of tampon usage and the toxic shock syndrome." *Postgraduate Medical Journal* Vol. 61, Supp. 1 (1985): pp. 31-3.

Freidrich, Eduard. "Tampon-Associated Vaginal Ulcerations." *Obstetrics & Gynecology* Vol. 55, No. 2 (February, 1980): pp. 149-56.

Friedman, Nancy. *Everything You Must Know About Tampons.* Berkley Books: New York, 1981.

———. "Tampon Effects on Vaginal Health." *Clinical Obstetrics and Gynecology* Vol. 24, No. 2 (June, 1981): pp. 395-405.

Gallert, Dale. U.S. Patent #4,475,911 (Absorbent Devices category). October 9, 1984. Assigned to Procter & Gamble Co., Cincinnati.

Geddes, Jennifer. Personal communication about Vancouver area sewage treatment. Summer, 1991.

Health Products Task Force, City of Toronto Department of Health. *Women's Health Products Study.* 1982.

Holmes, Hannah. "The Truth About Tampons." *Garbage, The Practical Journal for the Environment.* (November/December, 1990): pp. 50-5.

Horsman, Paul. "Garbage Kills." *BBC Wildlife.* August, 1985.

Johnson Cover, Trish. R.V. Anderson Associates, Ottawa. Personal communication. Spring, 1991.

Kern, Jean. Public health nurse, Sarnia, Ontario. Personal communication. Spring, 1991.

Kimberly-Clark Corporation. *Summary Annual Report*. Dallas: 1990.

Larsen, Bryan, et al. "Vaginal Microbial Flora: Composition and Influences of Host Physiology." *Annals of Internal Medicine* Vol. 96, Part 2 (1982): pp. 926-30.

Lucas, C.M., and Mendes, M.F. "A bacteriological survey of sanitary dressings, and development of effective means for their disposal." *Journal of Hygiene* Vol. 84 (1980): pp. 41-6.

Lucas, Zoë. Sable Island. Personal communication. Spring, 1991.

MacDonald, Helen. "Reusable Menstrual Pads." *Earthkeeper* Vol. 1, No. 6 (July/August, 1991): pp 24-9.

Natke, Ed. Former head of the Product-Related Disease Division (defunct), Health and Welfare Canada. Personal communication. Spring, 1991.

Newhook, Ronald. Health and Welfare Canada, Environmental Substances Division, Priority Substances Section. Personal communication. Spring, 1991.

Nickerson, C. "In 'wretched refuse,' he finds national symbol." *Cape Cod Times*, September 19, 1986.

Robbins, Ruth, et al. "Effect of Tampon Wraps on Production of Toxic Shock Syndrome Toxin 1." *Reviews of Infectious Diseases* Vol II, Supp. 1 (January/February, 1989): pp. S197-S202.

————. "Production of TSS Toxin 1 by Staphylococcus aureus as Determined by the Tampon Disk-Membrane-Agar Method." *Journal of Clinical Microbiology* Vol. 25, (August, 1987): p. 1446.

Roberts, Leslie. "More Pieces in the Dioxin Puzzle." *Research News* October 18, 1991: p. 322.

Sautner, Stephen. Researcher, Clean Ocean Action, New Jersey. Personal communication. Spring, 1991.

Schneider, W., and Sustmann, S. U.S. Patent #4,583,980 (Sanitary Hygiene Products Having Odor-Preventing Properties). April 22, 1986.

Spears, Tom. "Montreal: An island surrounded by a sewer." *The Ottawa Citizen*, October 6, 1991, p. E1.

Stephenson, R.C. Chairman, Association of Sanitary Protection Manufacturers, United Kingdom. Letter. April 24, 1991.

Svenska Rayon. "Svenska Rayon introduces a completely chlorine-free viscose fibre." Press release.

Tambrands Canada Inc. *Annual Report*. Lake Success, New York: 1990.

————. *The Everyday Earthguide*. Toronto: 1991.

Tierno, Philip. New York University Medical Center, New York.

Personal communication. Spring, 1991.

U.S. Department of Health and Human Services, Food and Drug Administration, Center for Devices and Radiological Health. *Measurement of Leachables From Tampons.* June 29, 1981.

Welsh, Bill. Health and Welfare Canada, Bureau of Radiation and Medical Devices, Chief, Pre-Market Review. Personal communication. Spring, 1991.

Whall, Tracey. Highland Creek Treatment Plant, Scarborough, Ontario. Personal communication. Spring, 1991.

Yin, Lillian. Food and Drug Administration, Ob-Gyn-Dental Devices Branch, Washington. Personal communication. Spring, 1991.

Chapter 6
Tampons, part two: Toxic shock syndrome—too high a price

Berkley, S.F. "The Relationship of Tampon Characteristics to Menstrual Toxic Shock Syndrome." *Journal of American Medical Association* Vol. 258, No. 7 (August 21, 1987): pp. 917-20.

Braiman-Lipson, Judy. President, Empire State Consumers Association, Rochester, New York. Personal communication. Spring, 1991.

Byrne, Kathleen. "Toxic shock syndrome still a threat, M.D. says." *The Globe and Mail,* January 29, 1990.

Clayton, A.J., et al. "Toxic Shock Syndrome in Canada." *Annals of Internal Medicine* Vol. 96, Part 2 (1982): pp. 881-2.

Consolidation of Medical Devices Regulations, under the Canadian Food and Drugs Act. September, 1990.

Costello, Alison, et al. *The Sanitary Protection Scandal.* London: Women's Environmental Network, 1989.

Cushman, Deborah. "A shocking incident." *The Des Moines Register,* July 5, 1991.

Delaney, J., et al. *The Curse: A Cultural History of Menstruation.* Revised edition. Urbana, Illinois: University of Illinois Press, 1988.

Dunn, Gladys. Mother of Alice Corman-Dunn, Sarnia, Ontario. Personal communication. Spring, 1991.

Ewan, P. Health & Welfare Canada, Laboratory Centre for Disease Control, Ottawa, Personal Communication. Spring, 1991.

Fischetti, V.A., et al. "Role of Air in Growth and Production of Toxic Shock Syndrome Toxin 1 by *Staphylococcus aureas* in Experimental Cotton and Rayon Tampons." *Reviews of Infectious Diseases* Vol. 11, Supp. 1 (January/February, 1989): pp. S176-81.

Food and Drug Administration. Medical Devices; Labelling for Menstrual

Tampons; Ranges of Absorbency; Final Rule. 21 CFR Part 801, U.S. Federal Register.

Friedman, Nancy. *Everything You Must Know About Tampons.* New York: Berkley Books, 1991.

Gallert, Dale. U.S. Patent #4,475,911 (Absorbent Devices Category), October 9, 1984. Assigned to Procter & Gamble, Cincinnati.

Health and Welfare Canada, Health Protection Branch. Information Letter to Doctors on Toxic Shock Syndrome, February 20, 1981.

————. Information Letter to Manufacturers and Distributors of Menstrual Tampons Re: Proposed Absorbency Labelling Requirements for Menstrual Tampons, I.L. No. 762, July 5, 1989.

————. "Menstrual Tampons—Toxic Shock Syndrome." Press release. November 1, 1990.

Henter, Thomas. Health and Welfare Canada, Evaluator, Pre-Market Review, Bureau of Radiation and Medical Devices. Personal communication. Spring, 1991.

Holmes, Hannah. "The Truth About Tampons." *Garbage, The Practical Journal of the Environment* (November/December, 1990): pp. 50-5.

Josey, Stan. "Tampon users told to beware of flu symptoms." *Toronto Star*, September 10, 1987, p. A14.

Kehoe, M. "Specialist is certain syndrome killed girl." *The London Free Press*, December 20, 1990.

Kimberly-Clark. *Summary Annual Report.* Dallas, Texas: 1990.

McKilligin, Helen. Ontario Ministry of Health, Senior medical consultant. Personal communication. 1987.

Oakie, Susan. "Teaching Young Women About Toxic Shock." *Washington Post*, July 31, 1985.

Ontario Ministry of Health. *Growing Up O.K.* Toronto: Queen's Printer, 1987.

Osterholm, M.T., et al. "Toxic Shock Syndrome." *Annals of Internal Medicine* Vol. 96, Part 2 (1982): pp. 954-8.

Public Citizen Health Research Group et al. v. Commissioner, Food and Drug Administration, (1989) 724 F. Supp. 1013 (U.S. District Court, District of Columbia).

Reingold, A.L. "Risk Factors for Menstrual Toxic Shock Syndrome: Results of a Multistate Case-Control Study." *Review of Infectious Diseases* Vol. 11, Supp. 1 (January/February, 1989): pp. S35-41.

Riggs, Richard, et al. "Awareness, Knowledge and Perceived Risk for

Toxic Shock Syndrome in Relation to Health Behavior." *Journal of School Health* Vol. 53, No. 5 (May, 1983): pp. 303-7.

Riley, Tom. *The Price of a Life: One Woman's Death from Toxic Shock.* Bethseda, Maryland: Adler & Adler, 1986.

Robbins, Ruth, et al. "Production of TSST-1 by *Staphylococcus aureus* as Determined by Tampon disk-Membrane-Agar Method." *Journal of Clinical Microbiology* (August, 1987).

Rome, Esther. Boston Women's Health Collective. Personal communication. Spring, 1991.

Rome, Esther, and Wolhander, Jill. "The Absorbency of Tampons." Letter to the editor of the *Journal of the American Medical Association* Vol. 259, No. 5 (February 5, 1988): pp. 685-6.

———. "Can Tampon Safety Be Regulated?" In *Menstrual Health and Women's Lives*, Alice Dan and Linda Lewis, eds. Champagne, Illinois: University of Illinois Press, 1991.

Sacks, Diane. "Junior tampons ideal for 12-year-old." *The Ottawa Citizen*, January 3, 1991, p. C3.

Sherrid, Pamela. "Tampons After the Shock Wave." *Fortune* (August 10, 1981): pp. 114-29.

Tambrands Canada Inc. *Accent on You.* Booklet. Toronto.

———. *Annual Report.* Lake Success, New York: 1990.

———. *The Inside Story: Facts about growing up.* Booklet. Toronto.

"Tampons: Less is More." *Canadian Consumer* Vol. 3 (1990): p. 7.

Tierno, Philip. New York University Medical Center, New York. Personal communication. Spring, 1991.

Tierno, Philip, and Hanna, B. "Ecology of Toxic Shock Syndrome: Amplification of TSS Toxin by Materials of Medical Interest." *Review of Infectious Diseases* Vol. 11, Supp. 1 (January/February 1989): pp. S182-S186

"Toxic Shock: A 'Success Story.'" *The New York Times*, September 4, 1988.

Verdict of the Coroner's Jury in the inquest into the death of Alice Corman-Dunn, Sarnia, Ontario. December 20, 1990.

Wager, Gael. "Toxic Shock Syndrome: A Review." *American Journal of Ostetrics and Gynecology* Vol. 146, No. 1 (May 1, 1983): pp 93-102.

Welsh, Bill. Health & Welfare Canada, Chief, Pre-Market Review, Bureau of Radiation and Medical Devices. Personal communication. Spring, 1991.

Witzig, Diane. Rochester, Minnesota. Personal communication. Spring, 1991.

Witzig, Diane, and Ostwald, Sharon. "Knowledge of Toxic Shock Syndrome Among Adolescent Females: A Need for Education." *Journal of School Health* Vol. 55, No. 1 (January, 1985): pp. 17-19.

Wolfe, Sidney. "Dangerous Delays in Tampon Absorbency Warnings." *Journal of the American Medical Association* Vol. 258, No. 7 (August 21, 1987): pp. 949-51.

Wolfe, Sidney, et al. *Women's Health Alert: What Most Doctors Won't Tell You About.* Redding, Mass: Addison-Wesley Publishing Company, 1991.

Women's Environmental Network. *Sanitary Protection: Women's Health and the Environment.* Pamphlet. 1991.

Wright, S.W., et al. "Toxic Shock Syndrome: A Review." *Annals of Emergency Medicine* Vol. 17, No. 3 (1988): p. 268.

Yin, Lillian. Food and Drug Administration, Ob-Gyn-Dental Devices Branch, Washington. Personal communication. Spring, 1991.

Young, James. Chief Coroner for Ontario, Ministry of the Solicitor General. Personal communication. Spring, 1991.

Chapter 7
Whitewash: Everything but the whole truth

Affidavit by Admiral E.R. Zumwalt, Jr., retired U.S. Navy, in the case of *Shirley Ivy* v. *Diamond Shamrock Chemical Company et al.* Case numbers: CV-89-03361 (EDNY)(JBW) and (B-89-00559-CA [EDTex]).

Cambridge Reports. *Confidential Paper Industry Study of Dioxin Issue,* on behalf of the American Paper Institute. June 1, 1987. Leaked to Greenpeace, September, 1987.

Chlorine Institute. Statement on the Use of Chlorine in the Pulp and Paper Industry—The Dioxin Issue. Washington: March, 1990.

Colodey, A.G., and Sinclair, W.F. "An Economic, Technical and Biological Review of the British Columbia Council of Forest Industries (COFI) Report: Sustainable Development and the B.C. Pulp and Paper Industry (March 1990)." Unpublished report for Environment Canada. June, 1990.

Darby, Dennis. Procter & Gamble, Manager, Environmental, Professional and Regulatory Services, Toronto. Letter to the Board of Health, City of Toronto, April 17, 1991.

Daschle, Thomas. "Agent Orange: 10 Years of Struggle." *The American Legion* Vol. 128, No. 2 (1989).

"The Diaper Discussion." *The New York Times,* February 24, 1991, p. F4.

Edelman Medical Communications. Letter/press release to the editor of *Scientific American* (December 5, 1990).

Gammie, Craig. Kimberly-Clark, Government affairs—Environmental. Letter to the Board of Health, City of Toronto. April 8, 1991.

Holloway, Margeurite. "A Press Release on Dioxin Sets the Record Wrong." *Scientific American* (April, 1991): p. 24.

Ketchum Communications. "Crisis Management Plan for The Clorox Company" (undated). Leaked to Greenpeace U.S.A., May, 1991.

Krauser, John. Ontario Medical Association, Association Director, Health Policy. Letter to the Board of Health, City of Toronto, April 12, 1991.

Montgomery, Wendy. Tambrands Canada, Director of Marketing, Letter. October 1, 1991.

"Nappy Claims Disputed." London *Guardian*, September 14, 1991.

"New York Challenges Procter & Gamble Ad on Disposable Diapers." *The Wall Street Journal*, March 13, 1991, p. B4.

Pickup, Carol. Councillor, Municipality of Saanich. Personal communication. Spring, 1991.

"Procter & Gamble Exposed." *Women's Environmental Network Newsletter* No. 12 (Autumn, 1991): pp. 1, 3.

"Recycling Council of Ontario urges action over disposable diaper ad." *Ontario Recycling Update* Vol. 11 (June, 1991): p. 1.

Rohleder, F. "Dioxins and Cancer Mortality—Reanalysis of BASF Cohort." Paper presented to the Ninth International Symposium on Chlorinated Dioxins and Related Compounds, Toronto. September, 1989.

Silbergeld, Ellen. Visiting Professor of Toxicology at the University of Maryland, Baltimore. Letter to Dr. Jan Witkowski, Director, Banbury Center, Cold Spring Harbor, New York, January 29, 1991.

Thornton, J., and Costner, P. *Science For Sale, a critique of Monsanto Studies on Worker Health Effects Due to Exposure to 2,3,7,8-tetrachloro-dibenzo-p-dioxin (TCDD)*. Washington: Greenpeace U.S.A., 1990.

U.S. Paper Industry Information Office. Sample media letter/Dioxin Fact Sheet, February 11, 1991. Faxed to authors from the Fraser Company, Edmunston, N.B.

Van Strum, Carol, and Merrell, Paul. *No Margin of Safety: A Preliminary Report on Dioxin Pollution and the Need for Emergency Action in the Pulp and Paper Industry*. Washington: Greenpeace U.S.A., 1987.

Zumwalt, Jr., E.R. *Report to the Secretary of the Department of Veterans Affairs on the Association Between Adverse Health Effects and Exposure to Agent Orange*. Washington: May 5, 1990.

Chapter 8
Ragtime revisited: The case for reusables

Boston Women's Health Collective. *The New Our Bodies, Ourselves.* New York: Simon and Schuster, 1984. p. 212.

Burrows, Lynn. Women's Choice, Gabriola, British Columbia. Personal communication. Spring and fall, 1991.

Crawford, Lou. The Keeper, Cincinnati. Personal communication. Summer, 1991.

Dadd, Debra Lynn. "Earthwise Feminine Protection Choices." *Environmental Action* (March/April, 1991): p. 9.

Delaney, J., et al. *The Curse: A Cultural History of Menstruation.* Revised edition. Urbana, Illinois: University of Illinois Press, 1988.

Drummer, Jan. We Care/Waddles in White, Hamilton, Ontario. Personal communication. Spring, 1991.

Fox, Sally. Wasco, California. Personal communication. Summer, 1991.

Hartley, Liann. Many Moons, Victoria, B.C. Letter. Winter, 1991.

Holmes, Hannah. "The Truth About Tampons." *Garbage, The Practical Journal for the Environment* (November/December, 1990): pp. 50-5.

Parvati, Jeannine. *Hygieia, A Woman's Herbal.* Freestone, 1978.

Smith, Eileen. Victoria, B.C. Personal communication. Summer, 1991.

Smith-Heavenrich, Sue. "Converting to Cloth." *Mothering* (Winter, 1991): pp. 44-5.

Slayton, Tamara. Executive Director, The Menstrual Health Foundation, Santa Rosa, California. Personal communication. Summer, 1991.

Webster, Donovan. "Reporter At Large: Heart of the Delta." *New Yorker* (July 8, 1991): pp. 44-66.

Chapter 9
How British women beat them on the bleaches

For more information about the Women's Environmental Network in Great Britain, contact Bernadette Vallely, WEN, Aberdeen Studios, 22 Highbury Grove, London, England N5 2EA. Telephone: 071 354 8832. Fax: 071 354 0464.

Chapter 10
The power of one, the glory of many

Cohen, Gary, and O'Connor, John. *Fighting Toxics.* Washington: Island Press, 1990.

Environment Canada. "Effluents from Pulp Mills Using Bleaching." *Priority Substances Assessment Report No. 2*. Ottawa: Queen's Printer, 1991.

Lamb, Marjorie. *Two Minutes a Day for a Greener Planet*. Toronto: HarperCollins Publishers Ltd, 1990.

Maathai, Wangari. "Foresters Without Diplomas." *Ms*. Vol. 1, No.5 (March/April, 1991): pp. 74-5.

May, Elizabeth. Sierra Club, Ottawa. Personal communication. Summer, 1991.

Miller, Doug. "Women and the Environment." Speech presented to Women and the Environment: Charting A New Environmental Course conference, Toronto, May, 1990.

Philip, John. Scott Paper, Vancouver. Letter. September, 1991.

Scott Paper. Advertisements in various consumer magazines, including *Canadian Living*.

Smythe, Donna. "Finding Out—The Rise of Citizen Science." From *Ideas* (radio series). Canadian Broadcasting Corporation, Toronto, 1985.

Statistics Canada. *Canadian Cancer Statistics 1991*. Toronto: National Cancer Institute of Canada, 1991.

Swain, W.R. Testimony before the Alberta-Pacific Environment Impact Assessment Review Board, Public Hearings Proceedings, Vol. 43. Edmonton, Alberta, December 4, 1989, p. 5880.

Wyman, Miriam. "Living the Questions—Environment from a woman's perspective." Speech presented to the Time for Action Conference, Toronto, January 24, 1990.

And finally...

Cohen, Gary and O'Connor, John. *Fighting Toxics*. Washington: Island Press, 1990.

Environment Canada. "Effluents from Pulp Mills Using Bleaching." *Priority Substances Assessment Report No. 2*. Ottawa: Queen's Printer, 1991.

Philip, John Scott Paper Ltd., Vancouver. Letter. September, 1991.

Statistics Canada. *Canadian Cancer Statistics 1991*. Toronto: National Cancer Institute of Canada, 1991.

Swain, W.R. Eco Logic, Ann Arbor, Michigan. Testimony before the Alberta-Pacific Environment Impact Assessment Review Board, Public Hearing Proceedings, Vol. 43. Edmonton, Alberta. December 4, 1989, p. 5880.

Index

Liz Armstrong, a writer and teacher, and Adrienne Scott, a lawyer practising environmental law, undertook this project under the auspices of the Toronto-based WEED Foundation (Women and Environments Education and Development Foundation).